THE Tofu Book

The New American Cuisine

John Paino & Lisa Messinger

AVERY PUBLISHING GROUP INC.

Garden City Park, New York

Photo Credits

Photos on pages 1, 2, 5, 23, and 41 reprinted courtesy of the American Soybean Association.

Photos on page 8 reprinted courtesy of Quong Hop & Company.

Cover Art and Design: Selame Design
Original Illustrations: Vicki Rae Chelf
In-House Editors: Joanne Abrams, Cynthia J. Eriksen, and
    Elaine Will Sparber

Library of Congress Cataloging-in-Publication Data

Paino, John.
    The tofu book : the new American cuisine / John Paino, Lisa Messinger.
        p.   cm.
    Includes bibliographical references.
    Includes index.
    ISBN 0-89529-409-5
    1. Cookery (Tofu) 2. Tofu   I. Messinger, Lisa, 1962–
II. Title.
TX814.5.T63P35   1991
641.6'5655—dc20   90-46079
                                                                             CIP

Copyright © 1991 by John Paino and Lisa Messinger

Printed in the United States of America

20 19 18 17 16 15 14 13 12 11

Contents

Acknowledgements

A book of this type—broad in scope and varied in content—could not be written without the help of many people. While it's impossible to thank everybody who contributed by providing information, reviewing text, lending photos, and generously offering their support and encouragement, a number of people must be mentioned—people without whom this book would never have been written.

First, thanks must go to Rudy Shur of Avery Publishing Group, who provided the original impetus for the creation of this book. Rudy's enthusiasm kept us going, while his expertise kept us on track.

Thanks, too, must go to the staff of Avery Publishing, particularly Joanne Abrams, Cynthia Eriksen, and Elaine Will Sparber, for their patient and diligent attention to detail throughout the editorial process.

When we first began work on *The Tofu Book*, Ellen Sue Spivack spent countless hours researching the history of tofu and helping us tell tofu's important story. Her work proved to be invaluable.

Thanks also must go to William Shurtleff and Akiko Aoyagi of Soyfoods Center. William and Akiko were kind enough to go over the history section with a fine-toothed comb, making sure that all of the many details of tofu's long and fascinating history were accurately related. We can't thank them enough for their help.

Mark Kempf of the American Soybean Association provided us with a dazzling array of original photos showing soybean cultivation and tofu making. Mark's photos have added immeasurably to our book by bringing the story of tofu alive.

Benwade Lee of Quong Hop & Co.—the oldest United States tofu shop still in existence—kindly provided us with photos of his family's original store, opened in 1906. We thank Benwade for allowing us to share with our readers this important period of tofu history.

We also wish to thank our friends at Selame Design who, having created the package design for the Nasoya family of products, transformed that great-looking motif for the cover of *The Tofu Book*.

We gratefully acknowledge the help of Sarah Paino, whose expertise in cooking made it possible to present you with this delicious collection of recipes. In this aspect of the book's production, as in many others, Sarah's help was invaluable.

Finally, we'd like to thank Vern Lawson, Don Hanson, Darlene Phillips, and the owners of the Antelope Valley Press, Lisa's base newspaper. Lisa also gives much thanks for their long-time support to Joel Weiss, Joan and Harold Messinger, Regina Messinger, and Robert Messinger and Dalia Hed-Ram.

John Paino
Lisa Messinger

Preface

T he idea for writing a book on tofu began four years ago at a summer camp at Simon's Rock College in the lovely Berkshire Mountains of Massachusetts. I was there with my wife, Sarah, having been invited to speak on the subject of starting your own business. Sarah had also been invited to teach a series of classes on natural foods cooking, featuring the use of tofu.

Between classes and lectures, an outdoor tent had been erected for companies to display some of their natural foods and publications. Sarah and I were at the Nasoya booth handing out samples when a young man approached the booth with a stack of natural foods cookbooks and other books on natural healing. He introduced himself as Rudy Shur, and we began to discuss the need for a comprehensive book on tofu that would help to bring this strange Oriental food to a wider market of people around the country. In a few minutes, we realized that we had a great deal in common, and that we might very well be able to work together—and have some fun to boot.

Within a few weeks, Rudy and I had hammered out the basic concepts behind this book, which was to include a number of chapters on tofu's history, tofu's health benefits, and the tofu-making process, as well as a substantial collection of recipes that would reflect the changes in eating habits that we felt were taking place across America. These changes, many of which were spawned by the overwhelming scientific evidence that indicted our heavy cholesterol and saturated-fat diets, had created a real demand for heart-healthy alternatives, and for this reason we felt the timing was perfect for the introduction of a new book on tofu. Rudy coined the phrase "the new American cuisine," which seemed to convey the result of those changes we saw taking place across America. And the book was born.

After a few false starts, we were extremely fortunate to get in touch with Lisa Messinger, who promptly agreed to head up the research and much of the historical and scientific background and writing that was needed to pull the book together. Then it just so happened that Nasoya's sales began to grow at a much faster clip than I had expected—and I'm not complaining—so that my time became less and less available for assisting in the difficult task of putting all the diverse pieces of information together into one unified whole. Lisa's work here was necessary and invaluable. Since Lisa lived on the West Coast and I on the East, we spent a few Sunday afternoons on the telephone, manuscripts in front of us, reviewing, inserting, deleting, and finally rewriting.

Even so, it was to be a year before Lisa and I met in person. The occasion was the Natural Foods Expo at Anaheim, California. I had just given a brief lecture on soy foods and the nineties, and Lisa, who I obviously didn't recognize, walked up and told me that she loved my lecture, loved our products, and had been a secret admirer of mine for a long time. Having had my ego stroked three times in the span of a few seconds was almost too much to bear, so I put on my debonair look and was just about to go back for more when I noticed a sly smile beginning to form across her face. After a few seconds, her smile widened completely, and she pointed to her conference badge, which read, "I'm Lisa Messinger." After we stopped laughing, I silently resolved not to be so gullible in the future.

With regard to the insets, I have tried to bring to the book a flavor of what it was like starting up a company in the late seventies, in a new industry, with a strange product that we nevertheless sensed would someday become as American as apple pie. I hope you enjoy reading them as much as I have enjoyed writing them and reliving some of the scenes I describe.

As far as the recipes go, well, you'll have to judge them for yourself. We have tried to bring you a wide variety of great-tasting dishes that are heart-healthy, and should also keep your weight down. We've included all kinds of ethnic dishes, such as tofu lasagna, tofu quiche, and various stir-fry dishes. And, of course, we've included many of your favorite American dishes—except that we've used tofu instead of meat or cheese. Try them. Change them to suit your tastes. Improve on them. They're just starting points from which you can use your own sense of flavor, texture, color, and presentation. Be creative! In the end, what really matters is that you begin to weave this wonderful food into the pattern of your everyday diet.

1. *TOFU IN TIME*
The History of Tofu

T he Buddhist missionaries from Korea and China who first transported the soybean to Japan between 200 and 700 A.D. probably never dreamed that they were starting a trend that would still be going strong over a thousand years later—and half a world away. But when a busy San Francisco couple pops a frozen tofu lasagna entrée into their microwave tonight; or health-conscious bicyclists whip up some pesto dip, ensalada de Aguacate, savory corn chowder, angel hair primavera, and coffee liqueur mousse (all made with tofu) for a quick dinner party; they—and thousands like them across the Western Hemisphere—prove that the movement that started with those first missionaries' steps is still gathering momentum.

When Sing Hau Lee left the Kwangtung Province in southern China for San Francisco in the 1880s and in 1906 opened Quong Hop and Company, the United States' first tofu shop still in existence, he probably didn't think that the food he sold to Asian railroad workers would eighty years later—along with the products of Nasoya and other tofu manufacturers—be a staple of mainstream supermarkets from Tennessee to Taiwan.

Similarly, when John Paino and his brother-in-law Bob Bergwall started Nasoya in 1978, they didn't realize they were sitting on the seeds of a multi-million-dollar business. They didn't expect that this

Cultivated first in ancient Korea and China, the soybean plant is now an important crop throughout the world.

The early history of tofu presented in this chapter was summarized with permission from *History of Tofu* by William Shurtleff and Akiko Aoyagi. Lafayette, California: Soyfoods Center, 1983.

The humble soybean has had a long and rich history.

"health food," tofu, which they had quietly begun making in a converted dairy barn in New England, would turn into a national phenomenon. In fact, by personally delivering their homemade tofu to the few New England markets that then carried the product, John and Bob had joined a new breed of pioneers in the history of tofu in the West. This followed almost a century on the heels of tofu pioneers like Sing Hau Lee.

Now, a little more than a decade later, you'll find a number of varieties of tofu prominently displayed on supermarket shelves all over America.

For years, food experts have been saying that tofu is the food of the future, and that its time will come. Obviously, with the emergence of frozen tofu entrées and traditional tofu cakes in our major supermarkets, that time is here now. Most of us have heard of tofu, but undoubtedly some who will see it for the first time in their local market may think it is a new product.

Tofu's rich history as a healthy food staple, however, shows that this couldn't be further from the truth. Tofu, as it is called in Japan and the United States; *doufu*, as it is known in China; *tahu*, as the Indonesians call it; and *tohu*, as it is called by the Burmese, has been a mainstay in the Orient for over two thousand years.

THE BIRTH OF TOFU IN CHINA

Tofu's invention in China may have been due to an overzealous cook's miscalculations with seasoning. Literature tells us that that cook may have been Lord Liu An or an earlier Chinese. One theory speculates on how tofu may have been born accidentally.

When soybeans, one of the Five Sacred Grains, were prepared, they most likely were dried first. Some cooks then soaked the beans and made them into a mashed concentrate, which they boiled. That purée would turn into a thick soup. After cooking the mixture, Liu An or the attendant cook might have removed the fibrous okara from the mixture to create a creamier texture.

When the soup had reached its desired texture, seasonings would have been stirred in. Some scholars note that if natural sea salt were added, because the salt contains nigari, which was later used as a coagulant in tofu production, curds would have formed. If the cook then drained off the resulting whey, the curds would have begun to become compressed under their own weight. In time, the curds would have molded themselves into a white, shimmering mass that would have resembled our modern-day tofu! An innovative cook may have found that the product kept fresh longer if submerged in its own whey—or, better yet, in cold water—and could later be sliced, cubed, or diced and used in any number of interesting dishes. So, the food that became a staple for millions may have gotten its start as an ancient kitchen mishap!

Some food historians have another guess as to how tofu may have arrived in China. This theory suggests that the Chinese may have actually been tutored in the method of preparing tofu. Since the Chinese did not, for the most part, use milk from cows or goats, the whole curdling process may have been foreign to them. At that time, however, curds and cheeses were being made by both the Indians to the south and the Mongols to the north. The method may have been picked up from observations of either of these two groups. Ideas from the outside regarding food were apparently acceptable to the Chinese, since they adapted many foreign recipes and imported a number of their favorite foods from other countries.

Throughout history, many food sources in China have been scarce. However, there has usually been a steady supply of soybeans. Once the Chinese knew how to prepare tofu, they made it a habit. Much as tofu is spreading like wildfire in the West today, it quickly found its way into the culture and cuisine of China. Beginning with the Ming Dynasty (1368–1662), when emperors made special requests for tofu dishes, and extending to the Chin Dynasty (1662–1912) and beyond, tofu was one of China's favorite foods.

Tofu, for thousands of years a staple in China, may originally have been the result of a culinary accident!

The Chinese believed that tofu gave them more than just a nutritional edge and a tasty dinner. One book described tofu as a healing food, one that cools and helps rid the body of toxins, is useful in cleansing the intestines, and even helps cure dysentery and jaundice. Today, tofu is still used throughout the East for medicinal as well as culinary purposes.

TOFU SPREADS TO JAPAN

Today, as in ancient times, tofu is valued throughout the Orient not only for its nutritional value, but also for its healing properties.

The actual word "tofu" did not appear in Japan until the 1500s. *Tofu Hyaku Chin*, the first book about tofu, was written in 1782, and contained numerous tofu recipes. Having lasting appeal, the book is still widely quoted.

Well before the publication of this famous book, those Buddhist monks who first carried soybeans from China to Japan used the high-protein food to sustain themselves, and even as a temple offering. Some historians speculate that the vegetarian monks were actually predecessors to the over 120 tofu shops in the United States today and over 30,000 shops in Japan by setting up tofu shops right inside the temples. As a matter of fact, it is thought that this practice made tofu fashionable among the rich, and expanded Buddhism in Japan. Around the fourteenth century, five major Zen temples opened up vegetarian public restaurants specializing in tofu.

In short order, tofu was virtually the national food of Japan. Popularity of the food led preparers' imaginations to concoct new and exciting dishes. Restaurants became exclusive. A fourteenth-century menu might have offered tofu soup, skewered tofu, tofu stew, dried frozen tofu, grilled tofu, silken tofu, and even tofu burgers. Those of us who might have thought tofu, tempeh (a bean cake made of cultured soybeans), or vegetarian burgers were creations of 1970s Western health food restaurants probably wouldn't have thought that a Japanese diner from the 1300s enjoyed the same dish.

In addition to the tofu preparation that was going on in Japanese restaurants, there was also a whole tradition being built around tofu making in the Japanese countryside. Scholars have compared the history of preparing this kind of tofu to that of homemade baking in America. In each Japanese village, there would be women working at home—maybe ten in each village—who had their own grinding stones and tofu-preparation tools. These women would get up hours before dawn and begin the handgrinding so that the tofu would be ready in the morning.

Later, tofu "masters" were to emerge, and would ritualize every aspect of tofu making, elevating the process almost to a religion. They had apprentices working with them who dreamed of one day becoming masters and having their own shops.

As home baking in the United States was eventually eclipsed by commercial baking, so did these Japanese home village tofu shops eventually become extinct. However, because tofu was considered a delicacy in the villages, the women home preparers played an important part in the food's history and continuing acceptance for many years.

When the tofu shops did open in Japan, the tofu "masters" took exceptional pride in their work and surroundings. Quality was placed above all else. Only flawless cakes were tolerated by the master.

The traditional craftsman appeared each morning in his raised wooden *geta*, much like a wooden clog shoe, which kept his feet dry by lifting him above any wetness on the floor. His apron bore letters describing his lineage. The wooden tools and baskets that were used to make the tofu were kept exceptionally clean, and one day a week was taken off so that everything could be cleaned to perfection.

In Japan, tofu is still stored in traditional stone vats.

In traditional Japan, the tofu master viewed tofu making as more an art form than a science, and considered his work to be a spiritual path toward self-realization.

The Japanese craftsman considered his work to be a spiritual path, or *sadhana*, toward self-realization. Inner peace and artistic excellence in creating his tofu were primary goals. The whole process was about much more than just tofu, much more than just food. In fact, throughout the centuries, tofu making has carried the same special pride for many tofu makers. Even now, because of tofu's special history, its manufacture is considered more of an art form, like fine wine making, than a science. When tofu makers get together, they may speak in general terms about the process, but there is an underlying understanding that the details and special procedures are never discussed. These secrets took years to uncover. They are the family jewels. They create the differences between one brand of tofu and another.

TOFU SPREADS TO THE WEST

So how did this culturally special Eastern food—once made only by Eastern tofu masters—make its way into the West? One theory has tofu travelling home from China with European traders and missionaries during the sixteenth century. But, although tofu was mentioned by Domingo Navarrete, an Italian friar, in 1665, it was not until 1859 that a European, a prominent French seedsman, was recorded as making tofu in Europe.

During the last part of that century and into the start of the twentieth century, the French conducted nutritional analyses on tofu, as did the Germans and the Russians. But, it was left to a Chinese living in Paris to receive the world's first patent for tofu. In 1910, Li Yu-Ying developed such innovative and tasty specialties as tofu sausages, and was granted the patent by Great Britain.

Ultimately, though, it was an attention-catching slogan that really got tofu's popularity off the ground in the West. Around 1920, a Western chemistry professor living in China coined the catchy phrase "the meat without bones" to describe tofu. With its essence succinctly captured for perhaps the first time, people better understood the importance of tofu, and it gained popularity with certain groups across the country.

Since there was no full-fledged ongoing campaign behind the professor's catchy slogan, however, popular interest in tofu eventually waned—until the 1970s, when it became a darling of the health food circuit in the United States. It was well before that health-concerned decade, however, that tofu made the migration to America.

As Chinese immigrants looked to the United States for work, eventually becoming busy laborers, the art of ancient tofu making was bound to be tucked in along with the other valuables that they brought on the journey with them.

The first writings about tofu in the United States appeared around 1896. And large cities that had significant Oriental populations probably had at least one tofu shop. Some of these were quite informal. Many of the Orientals ended up as railroad workers, and card and gossip groups gathered around the tracks, where freshly made tofu was sold. Chinese groceries in the United States that served these hard laborers were not depending solely on American wares. They were importing traditional Chinese products—among them, the ingredients for tofu.

Soon, Chinese restaurants and laundries were gracing the cities, as laborers found it harder to find work on the railroads, and migrated into these service industries. As Gold Rush-era Californians, and others in cities that boasted large Oriental populations, feasted on exotic dishes in these Chinese restaurants, probably few guessed that many of their favorites were made with tofu or, as it is sometimes called, bean curd.

Just as many of us today can name our favorite Chinese dish—Moo Shu Pork or Moo Goo Gai Pan—without being able to name its precise ingredients, this was most likely the case with visitors to those early Chinese restaurants. And, as Chinese restaurants began dotting the whole country in the 1950s, few diners probably were aware that they were boosting the tofu consumption in this country, let alone able to identify the word, if they were pressed to, on a pop quiz.

In 1906, well before Chinese restaurants became a favorite of United States diners, a Chinese immigrant named Sing Hau Lee opened Quong Hop and Company in San Francisco. This is considered the country's first tofu shop still in existence. Sing Hau Lee had left the Kwangtung Province in southern China in the 1880s and brought along his talent for tofu making. His shop made tofu daily and supplied the Asian rail workers with a delicacy they no longer felt they had left thousands of miles behind.

"In those days, Quong Hop [which means "Great Unity"] was like a Chinese general store," says Benwade Lee, Sing Hau's grandson, and the vice president for marketing of Quong Hop and Company. It is still a tofu manufacturer, making the now-popular food daily. Stanley, Benwade's father, is the president of the company, and his other children—Danwade, Kenwade, and Connie—all work in the business.

It was not Sing Hau, however, who received the first United States patent for tofu. That happened in 1916, when a man from

Photographs to the right and below show Quong Hop & Company as it appeared to its Oriental clientele in San Francisco during the early 1900s.

Seattle, Kameichi Murakami, applied. However, although clusters of Chinese immigrants were enjoying tofu, most non-Oriental Americans had not discovered tofu at the time of the First World War.

Dr. Yamue Kin, a woman physician and dietitian, tried to change all that. Continuing the line of important women in the history of tofu, Kin became a one-woman publicity campaign for what she saw as a very significant food. First, she launched a successful campaign for tofu that included experiments in cooperation with the United States Department of Agriculture. Kin also established a tofu plant and a restaurant that served a myriad of soy foods, and had her recipes printed in the 1923 classic book *The Soybean*.

Following up on Kin's work, in 1926 two more Americans, Rose and Macleod, conducted the country's first official nutrition study on tofu. It was in this study that tofu received some of its first recognition as a food that was very high in protein.

In Rose and Macleod's study, the protein content of soy foods was compared with that of such American staples as milk, meat, and bread. The first good health news regarding tofu appeared after these studies: Tofu was a complete protein, comparing very favorably with other foods.

By 1930, many companies had opened up shop in Chinatowns all over the continental United States and even in Hawaii. Tofu got another promotional boost at about this time when the Seventh-Day Adventists became the first Caucasian Americans to be recorded as taking up the ancient practice of tofu making. Because this religion encourages a vegetarian diet, the Seventh-Day Adventists wanted a food that could replace meat without totally abandoning its taste and texture. They found that food in tofu, and successfully introduced it to many non-Orientals. Today, several Adventist tofu products are still widely used.

During the Great Depression, the thoughts of Americans were, for the most part, otherwise occupied, and interest in tofu waned. However, as the country moved toward World War II—the time just before many of today's tofu-loving baby boomers were born—a renewed interest in soy foods, including tofu, emerged.

Leave it to automotive genius Henry Ford to take on the cause of tofu and soybeans. He is noted as one of the greatest proponents of these foods. Patriotism was on Ford's mind when he suggested that farmers produce industrial goods from farm products. Soybeans were at the top of his list when it came to those products.

This was about the time that the great versatility—not to mention nutritional value—of soy foods was beginning to be appreciated in the United States. Soy products were being sent overseas as part of a lend-lease program with our allies. While dairy and meat products were too costly and perishable to ship, soy meal, soy oil, and soybeans were not. Whether soybeans were an industrial commodity or a protein substitute, their importance could not be denied.

Tofu as a substitute for cottage cheese? That's what a 1943 *Science Newsletter* article suggested. And, after the war, there were more articles and research done on both the nutritional value of tofu and the tofu industry. But soon, as America began its 1950s love affair with milk and meat, tofu was forced behind the closed doors of Oriental homes and into the underground.

Of course, there was an increase in the popularity of Chinese restaurants in the United States during this time. The People's Republic of China was founded in 1949, and as many restaurants in China were closed, a number of chefs, fleeing west, found their food to be an immediate hit with Americans. Those little white blocks of bean curd—tofu—were a smash as they soaked up whatever flavoring was added to them.

Obviously, those 1950s Chinese chefs never thought that the next group to embrace tofu would be a cavalcade of long-haired, philosophical young people dubbed hippies. But, in fact, hippies ushered soy foods into the 1960s, where these foods would become widely accepted and recognized. It was the hippies on the famous Farm, a commune in Tennessee, who created Ice Bean, the first ice cream made without dairy products. Ice Bean was a precursor of Tofutti, and now both can be found in supermarkets throughout the nation.

Automotive genius Henry Ford was one of the United States's earliest proponents of soy foods. So enthusiastic was Ford that in addition to eating soybeans, he also wore a suit made entirely of soybean fibers!

It was about this time that John and Bob, as well as many others, began to think wholistically about the Earth, our farming practices, and the foods we were eating. Vegetarianism and the Eastern practice of macrobiotics—a vegetarian grain- and vegetable-based diet—were embraced. Their association with Zen Buddhism appealed to the counterculture as part of its infatuation with Eastern philosophies, and enticed health-oriented people toward a unique path to wellness. Many also appreciated that this delicious way of eating rice, seaweed, and soy foods was economical as well as environmentally sound.

Soon, tofu began appearing in tubs in health food stores and restaurants. George Ohsawa, considered the founder of modern macrobiotics, promoted the commercial sale of tofu. Berkeley Co-Op Systems, the first non-Oriental chain food store to sell tofu, sold a brand made by the tofu company Azumaya. By 1970, the two-thousand-year-old food, under the Azumaya label, was centrally located on the shelves of Safeway stores. By 1982, the company had surprised even itself by producing a whopping 110,000 pounds of tofu weekly.

Still, tofu had an image problem. It was considered a food for Americans of Oriental descent or a fad of vegetarians or hippies, not a sensible health alternative for mainstream Americans.

Tofu was hip. Tofu was trendy. But it appealed to a subculture, not the mass culture.

Then, in 1971, Frances Moore Lappe's *Diet for a Small Planet* hit the bookstores. As the millions who have read it know, Lappe branded the modern American diet—high in meat and fat—as unhealthy, unecological, uneconomical, and lacking consciousness in terms of world hunger. Her book and others that followed had the mass-media impact of luring millions of Americans away from a meat-centered diet, now considered to be destructive to their health.

In other words, the country's eyes were finally being opened. The recipes in *Diet for a Small Planet* and other related books popularized complementary proteins. They used rice and beans, tofu and grains, and other non-meat combinations as a superior source of protein.

When William Shurtleff and Akiko Aoyagi's *The Book of Tofu* was released at the end of 1975, the stage was already set for tofu. Both vegetarians and non-vegetarians were looking for a new, healthier, ecologically sound food, and tofu was the answer. It was a complete protein. It had no cholesterol. It was economical. And, as soon as tofu increased in popularity, tofu-making kits became available in natural food stores. Homemade bread, granola toasting, and tofu concocting all seemed to fall in line with the health movement of the times.

Now, even mainstream Weight Watchers, in its million-seller cookbooks, promotes tofu recipes. And the macrobiotic movement is stronger than ever in this country. Michio and Aveline Kushi on the East Coast, and Herman and Cornelia Aihara on the West Coast (all disciples of George Ohsawa) provide guidance and leadership. With macrobiotics, tofu and other soy foods, such as miso and tamari, have become even more popular. Eating lower on the food chain (toward plant foods and away from animals that eat plants) is no longer seen as unusual. From the United States Department of Agriculture (USDA), to Weight Watchers, to most cholesterol-conscious shoppers, a meat-centered diet is viewed as being less healthy.

Take a look at what the government has renamed the Standard American Diet: SAD. Everyone is recommending foods lower in fat and cholesterol, salt and sugar, and calories. Statistics show us the scary toll that SAD has taken on our population. But if you are nutrition conscious, let Chapter Two reinforce the nutritional clout of tofu.

If you're concerned about taste, seaweed still doesn't appeal to you, and you're trying to wean yourself from some of those not-so-healthy foods, take heart: Tofu can be a great transitional food. The recipes included in this book should be enticing, but if you still need convincing, think of tofu as a meat-textured sponge. What's your favorite flavor? Add it to tofu, and the tofu will take on that flavor without providing a calorie-, fat-, or sodium-laden base. A search through your supermarket may turn up tasty tofu treats: non-dairy ice cream products, tofu chili, tofu lasagna, tofu ravioli, tofu dips, even tofu hot dogs. It's remarkable!

Think of tofu as the food magician. It can trick and tempt your tastebuds by becoming almost anything you want it to be. It can trick you into thinking it's a new taste sensation, when it's really centuries old. Don't cut out tacos, chili, lasagna, pizza, and other treats—simply, deliciously, magically remake them with tofu. We'll show you how.

Tofu, which has earned its title as "the food magician," can be used deliciously—and healthfully—in tacos, chili, lasagna, pizza, and many of your other favorite foods.

Perhaps tofu is on its way to becoming so ingrained and popular in our society that someday we'll have sayings and proverbs as the Chinese and Japanese have concerning their precious food. In China, for example, finding fault with someone is compared to "finding a bone in your tofu." And, when the Japanese wish to tell someone to "get lost," they say, "Go bump your head against the corner of a tofu cake and drop dead."

Obviously, with the surge of tofu in the West, we already know that there are absolutely no "bones" to be found in tofu. We know that it's a soft, malleable, nutritious haven—nothing hard enough to "bump your head" on—and certainly an increasingly popular food that will never "get lost" again.

The Journey

Sitting on an outcropping of dense greenery and cool volcanic rock, I gazed at the scene before me. Bright shimmering carp, moving leisurely among the water lilies, created small wavelets across the surface of the pond. The smell of pine needles and moist leaves drifted down from the forests, settling in a thin mist. After sitting for a few moments and enjoying this lovely place, I shifted my weight to a more comfortable position. The stone beneath me was irregular, but I noticed it had been worn smooth, perhaps by those who had come to this place before me to enjoy the serenity of the natural setting. I wondered how many had also come, as I had today, to sample the legendary tofu cuisine.

It is a Buddhist belief that all living things are inextricably connected to each other, and that to kill another sentient being, even for food, will ultimately create suffering for oneself. Over the centuries, these Buddhist monks have embraced tofu as the protein backbone of their diets, and have developed its cuisine to such an art that numerous tofu restaurants, such as the one I had come to visit, can be found nestled in the foothills surrounding this ancient city. It once was a city of religious devotion, a city where pilgrims came to pray in the more than 1,500 temples and 500 shrines that reached toward the heavens. This was the ancient capital city of Kyoto.

The afternoon sun filtered through a break in the trees, its diffused rays softly illuminating the mist that had been rising above the pond. On a low stone table before me were two elegantly prepared tofu dishes. In one, the tofu had been charcoal broiled, carefully placed on bamboo skewers, and delicately seasoned with a spicy barbecue sauce. The other was presented in a small earthenware bowl and was surrounded by mushrooms, onions, and vegetables. In keeping with tradition, the tofu had been made before dawn by the tofu master. The taste was subtly sweet, almost imperceptibly so, but like so much of the Japanese culture, it was this very subtleness and mysteriousness that was so alluring.

What had always intrigued me about the art of making tofu was the sense of ritual and form that had evolved around it. I began to think about the tofu master rising before dawn and beginning his daily rituals—stone grinding the beans, cooking the purée, filtering the hulls, pressing the curds, cutting the blocks. And gradually, as these associations came to mind, the boundaries of time and space disappeared. I began to think back. . . .

The year was 1979. It was before dawn, and the New England winter winds swept fiercely across the open fields. Inside our small tofu shop, the familiar sounds of the early morning preparations echoed from every corner of the cold cinder-block room. The steam, rising from our open cauldrons, thickened the room with a dense fog. Visibility was limited to less than ten feet.

Bob, my partner and future brother-in-law, would begin preparing each batch of tofu by bringing well water to a boil, stone grinding the soybeans, and cooking the mixture for fifteen minutes. It was a task that demanded full attention; in seconds, the rising foam could explode like a volcano over the top of the kettle, sending us scurrying in all directions away from the boiling mass. I held that image for a few seconds and smiled to myself. It is one thing to have a pot boil over on your kitchen stove, and quite another to be standing beside a 200-gallon five-foot-high kettle when it erupts. I could vividly recall Bob, intent upon escaping, turning quickly, like some fleeing bandit, and firing a hose from over his shoulder to blast the rising foam in an attempt to subdue it.

Later, when the cooking process was complete, I would wait at the curding station for the hot soy milk to be pumped through the filtering bag that would separate the soy milk from the ground hulls. To each batch, I would add the coagulant nigari. The curding paddle would go around four times in a clockwise direction, and then abruptly stop as the nigari was poured down the long shaft. During the next thirty-two minutes, at eight-minute intervals, a precise method of coagulation was employed. An exact amount of nigari would be added until, at the very end of the process, the shimmering curds would be brought up from the bottom of the cauldron by the paddle and "voilà," the batch would be complete. Any deviation from this method would lose yield, consistency, or taste, jeopardizing the entire batch. Each day, Bob and I made ten batches, and it would be late evening before we were finished cleaning our equipment.

The work was long and arduous. Unable to afford suitable equipment, we were forced to put together a makeshift system using only Yankee ingenuity and dogged determination. To press the tofu, we used six five-gallon pails filled with water, and individually lifted them on and off each twenty-five-pound box hundreds of times every day. To remove the near-boiling curds and whey, we had to reach over the four-foot-high walls of the steaming cauldrons and lift them out using a five-gallon stainless steel bucket. Nevertheless, the work was deeply satisfying in an inexplicable way. People who visited our shop were amazed at what they saw. As if in some alchemist's laboratory, they stood in awe, witnessing the transformation of soybeans into a remarkable protein food called "tofu."

Our goal was to Americanize tofu, to introduce this wonderful food to as many people as possible. We knew that the diets of Americans were too rich in saturated fats and cholesterol, and that tofu could be used as an alternative to foods rich in these potentially harmful substances. We looked at tofu as a new food, just as yogurt was viewed not too long ago. Whereas yogurt is a traditional Middle Eastern food, tofu is a traditional Far Eastern food. Both have sustained millions of people for thousands of years. These foods are not fads; they are here to stay. They have been assimilated into our culture. After all, America is a melting pot of cultures.

It took us six long years, but eventually we were producing 25,000 pounds of tofu per week out of that 1,200-square-foot building. We processed tofu twenty-four hours a day, six days a week. There was no relief in sight. We needed more equipment, but we didn't want to go to Japan to get it. We wanted to design a system that was uniquely American. We hired an engineer, and we paid him to design a new system based on our existing process, which we had proudly developed using Yankee equipment and Yankee ingenuity. After reviewing his plans, however, we decided we had better start practicing our Japanese.

The problem was that to achieve a certain volume, you couldn't use the same methods that work in a small-scale tofu shop. The forces at work were too great. The American way is to take great big steps. The Japanese way is to take lots of tiny little steps. Guess which way works better for tofu making?

After one look at the brochures from a Japanese tofu machinery maker, we knew our home-grown Yankee virginity was lost forever. I laughed to myself. I was thinking of when we first met Mr. Sato, the owner of the company that ultimately was to provide us with our new equipment. It was a culmination of a thousand years of separation, East from West. It happened at the New Otuni Hotel in Los Angeles. We had flown 3,000 miles to meet Mr. Sato and to make a deal. Bob and I told him what we thought we needed. Mr. Sato listened quietly and then, leaning forward, he asked us if we really knew how to make tofu. He told us that if someone used his equipment to make inferior tofu, it would reflect badly on him. Bob was taken aback. He had been in charge of production, and was proud of his accomplishments. Bob leaned forward and said, "Mr. Sato, we would like to purchase your equipment for our new factory. Do you want to sell it to us or not?" Mr. Sato then said that we must come to Japan and study tofu making from his staff, using his equipment, and visiting factories where his equipment was installed. At this, Bob slammed his fist on the table, saying that we had no time to go to Japan, and that we needed the equipment immediately. Mr. Sato leaned back and smiled. I'll never forget his next words and how they left us dumbfounded. Leaning forward again, he said very softly, very deliberately, "Anything rushed comes to no good." End of discussion.

Two weeks later, Bob, my wife Sarah, and I were on a flight headed halfway around the world.

Slowly, I became aware of the scene before me. The afternoon sun had set behind the western hills, casting long shadows over the valley. We would return to our Japanese-style boarding house for dinner and a hot bath. In the morning, we planned to visit a tofu shop in the business section of the city. Later, we would walk to a Buddhist temple situated in the southernmost hills, among the pines. As we made our way through the tiny streets that led down the hill to the river, we noticed the mist descending over the temple roofs below.

2. *TOFU FOR HEALTH*
A Wise Alternative for a Better Diet

F amed health writer and best-selling nutrition author Jane Brody of *The New York Times* calls it a "nutritional wonder."

Janet and Peter Holmes, a young couple living in Tennessee, say that they are beginning to feel the same way Brody does about tofu.

Peter, a financial consultant in his mid-thirties, recently discovered that, although he thought he was eating a relatively low-fat diet, his cholesterol level registered at just over an unhealthy 300. After acting on his doctor's suggestion that he try eating tofu a few times a week, as well as making some other dietary modifications, Peter found that his cholesterol level had dropped to 220.

Peter and Janet say that they had always been interested in healthful eating, and became more concerned than ever when their daughter was born about two years ago. They are also food "adventurers" who like to try ethnic dishes like Chinese, Thai, Russian, Indian, and Korean.

Until recently, Janet and Peter never gave much thought to tofu. Now, however, they enjoy it at least two to three times a week as a satisfying cholesterol-fighting replacement in almost all of their former meat, poultry, cheese, and egg recipes. With ease, they can make dishes like tofu enchiladas, tofu kabobs, and tofu pizza. They are also beginning to see tofu as an important health ingredient in some of their favorite ethnic cooking adventures.

The Holmes family has obviously joined the rapidly growing ranks of health-conscious Americans who say they feel as if they see a "nutritional green light" flash on as they learn more about the tremendous health benefits of tofu.

We know that tofu has had a long and honored history, but with the nutrition-conscious wave in this country in full swing, it is as though millions of savvy consumers are discovering a whole new chapter about the nutritional benefits of tofu, and about how easy and tasty it is to include tofu in everything from quick-fix meals to gourmet sit-down dinners.

Over a decade ago, in April 1978, when Nasoya was established, the first year of sales registered at $60,000. By the second year, sales had risen to $200,000. By the third, $600,000 was the annual sales figure. And, recently, sales ran into the millions. Supermarket produce buyers, who for years had to be courted by Nasoya sales personnel, now routinely ask them, "What else do you have for me? We want more products. Our shoppers are concerned about their health."

The growth of total national tofu sales—including *only* tofu, and no tofu-based products—has been just as impressive. According to the Soyfoods Center of Lafayette, California, retail sales of tofu have grown steadily over the years, increasing from $19.7 million in 1978 to about $100 million in 1989. In fact, this country's acceptance of soy-food products as a whole has been nothing short of spectacular. In 1975, only 44 new soy-food products were introduced to the United States market. In 1987, more than 405 new soy-food products were introduced. Evidently, tofu and its soy cousins are here to stay!

Millions of health-conscious consumers have made "cholesterol" a national buzz word. Recently, two books that explain how to lower cholesterol simultaneously rose to fame on the best-seller lists. In their quest for better health, many have thrown out their salt shakers in favor of nutritious and delicious salt-free herbs and spices. In search of low-fat, quality protein foods, they have, for the first time, made the combined sales of chicken and turkey equal to those of beef products. It is not uncommon for people to discard cholesterol-laden egg yolks, and make lower cholesterol omelets with, perhaps, one yolk and three egg whites.

It is no wonder, then, that you and others with nutrition savvy are filling more and more shopping carts with tofu and tofu-based convenience products. As shown in the table on page 17, *tofu has absolutely no cholesterol*. It is very low in sodium. And, although it is high in energy-boosting protein—and a terrific meat, poultry, and cheese replacement—it is quite low in fat. The fat that tofu has is monounsaturated and polyunsaturated, the "good fats" that are not harmful to blood vessels. Tofu is also high in calcium, and is a good source of important vitamins and minerals.

A CHOLESTEROL COUNTER'S BEST FRIEND

Tofu isn't a medicine, but for some people—like Peter Holmes, who tried it on his doctor's advice—it may be one of the best and most delicious "medicines" in the war against cholesterol.

Cholesterol, as many of us have learned, is a chemical that our body uses to manufacture new cells and a number of hormones. The body makes all the cholesterol it needs. Therefore, if we add more cholesterol through the foods we eat, this excess cholesterol accumulating in the blood can be harmful. Cholesterol is one of the primary causes of heart disease—the number one killer in the United States.

Cholesterol can cause heart disease by building up in the walls of the arteries that supply blood to the heart muscle. This results in a condition known as arteriosclerosis. The arteries can become more and more clogged. And even a small amount of build-up is significant, since the arteries are so small. Most excess cholesterol in the body comes directly from our diet—whether through the marbled fat in beef, through egg yolks, or through other fatty foods.

Lately, we have heard a lot about "good" cholesterol and "bad" cholesterol. Actually, this refers to the particles that carry cholesterol

Nutritional Analysis of Protein-Rich Foods

4 oz. (112 gm.) portions	Protein gm.	Calories	Calories /gm. of protein	Cholesterol gm.	Fat gm.	Sodium mg.	Iron mg.	Calcium mg.
Tofu*	11.7	114	9.7	0	6.8	2.5	2	57.2
Milk, whole	3	62	20.7	16	3	56	.05	132
Cheddar cheese	28	455	16.25	118	37	784	0.8	840
Cottage cheese, 4% fat	14	116	8.3	17	5	256	.15	105
Egg, poached	13	179	13.8	1232	13	137	2.2	62
Tuna, canned in oil, drained	32	226	7.0	125	9	46	2.1	9
Chicken, boneless, white	37	227	6.1	108	13	72	1.5	12
Hamburger, 21% fat	27	321	11.9	96	23	82	3.5	12
Steak, broiled, sirloin	32	291	9.1	93	36	79	2.9	11

Source: Anderson, et al., *Health and Disease*, Seventeenth Edition. New York: Lippincott, 1983.
* The tofu analyzed here is extra firm style.

around in the bloodstream. LDL, low density lipo-proteins, or "bad" cholesterol, travels in the bloodstream, and some LDL is deposited in the walls of the arteries. HDL, high density lipo-proteins, or "good" cholesterol, actually helps remove bad cholesterol from the arteries and dispose of it.

When you get your cholesterol tested, it's important to know the ratio of HDL to LDL (and to have as much HDL as possible). Generally, a good cholesterol count is considered to be the number of one's age plus 100. A reading of 200 to 239 is considered borderline high, and readings of 240 and above are considered dangerous.

Although most of us now realize that high cholesterol is a potential killer, many people do not realize that cholesterol is found only in foods of animal origin. Foods that are vegetable based like tofu do not contain cholesterol. Therefore, even though tofu is a source high in protein, ranking with steak, chicken teriyaki, or fried eggs, it has none of the health-endangering cholesterol of those or other animal foods. And, it may also actually help to lower cholesterol in our bodies.

This is welcome news to all of us, since doctors generally recommend that cholesterol in the diet be limited to 300 milligrams each day. The average American daily diet has been estimated to contain an unhealthy 450 to 600 milligrams.

Cholesterol-free tofu may actually help to *lower* your cholesterol level!

So, how can tofu actually help to lower your cholesterol level? Two substances present in tofu—lecithin and linoleic acid—actually assist the body in lowering cholesterol levels by helping to break down cholesterol and fat deposits in the organs and blood. Experiments in the United States, Canada, Italy, West Germany, and France have shown that soybeans—and derivatives of them—help in this process.

Hypocholesterolemia is the term that has been coined to describe the effect that foods like tofu have on cholesterol. This means that tofu and foods like it are actually helpful in fighting cholesterol. In one study, described by Richard Leviton, author of *Tofu, Tempeh, Miso, and Other Soyfoods*, hospital patients who were given a soy-increased diet experienced a 20 percent decline in plasma cholesterol in just two weeks. In another study in which soy was increased in the diet, cholesterol levels dropped by thirty points in just fourteen days.

In an effort to reduce some of this country's biggest killers—heart disease, high blood pressure, and arteriosclerosis—doctors have virtually pleaded with the public to reduce the amount of animal protein that they consume. They might be better off, though, taking the route of Peter Holmes' doctor. Instead of telling people which foods they'll have to do without, they should let them in on a cholesterol-fighting, delicious, versatile food like tofu.

A DIETER'S DREAM

About 80 million Americans—one in three—are dieting at any given time. And, yet, obesity rates in this country are still escalating, rather than declining.

Most people on a weight-reduction diet know that large portions of protein foods like beef (juicy 16-ounce steaks), pork (sizzling pork ribs or pork chops topped with apple sauce), lamb, and even poultry with skin are not a dieter's best friend. But what high-protein foods *can* a dieter eat? Welcome to the "New Age" of tofu! Here is a protein food that is low in calories and saturated fat. It will give you the energy boost you need from protein, while at the same time absorb all the delicious spices, sauces, or dressings with which you serve it. It can "pretend" to be some of its high-calorie, high-fat counterparts, while you won't have to pretend that your excess weight is falling away.

When cooked with tofu, chili, lasagna, tacos, pizza, or even cheesecake can become a virtual "diet" food. In equal servings, tofu has 25 percent to 50 percent less calories than beef, and 40 percent less calories than eggs. A typical 4-ounce serving of extra firm tofu has less than 120 calories. This is truly a lean fuel for your body.

Some dieters crave cheese—a generally high-fat food that may contribute to excess weight. Because tofu is made like cheese, it can be a low-calorie alternative. Presently, concerned manufacturers like Nasoya are providing the marketplace with tasty products like Chinese 5 Spice Tofu and French Country Herb Tofu. The French Country Herb Tofu, in particular, cuts, looks, and tastes much like an herbed French cheese.

Look at the following calorie comparisons. A 4-ounce portion of cheddar cheese—also high in sodium—contains 455 calories. However, the same serving of most tofus has just 114 calories, and very little sodium!

LET'S TALK FAT

Obviously, any dieter or health-conscious person will take into consideration the fat and calorie content of the foods he consumes. And, as some people are now aware, recent research points to the fact that all calories are definitely *not* the same. Studies show that calories derived from fatty foods are much more likely to be stored as fat than are calories derived from nonfat foods. Calories from less fatty foods, like carbohydrates, are much more likely to be burned off as fuel. So, in fact, the result of eating 100 calories of bread or vegetables will most likely be different from that of munching on 100 calories of deep-fried chicken or pastry.

And, of course, there's a difference between the fats a food may contain. As we mentioned before, the fat in tofu is "good fat," polyunsaturated fat, that does not harm blood vessels. Therefore, although in tofu some of the calories come from fat, this is not considered to be harmful when compared with animal protein, which contains unhealthy saturated fats.

The average hamburger, for example, is at least 10 percent saturated fat. (And it's best not to get carried away by the notion that we can just "trim the fat" from our cuts of meat. Quite a bit of saturated fat is in the marbling we see within the meat, and cannot be trimmed away.) In comparison, most tofu has a total fat content of just 4.3 percent, a good percentage of which is not saturated.

It is generally not culprits like refined sugar that are responsible for most of the obesity in this country. Rather, it is the saturated fats found in meats like beef that cause food enthusiasts to gain unwanted pounds.

Therefore, any eating program that lowers fat intake—specifically, saturated fat intake—will most likely result in lost pounds and, perhaps, even add years to your life. Most of us, whether dieting or not, realize that the quality of what we eat affects our daily energy levels. Do we rush off eagerly to work, or do we wish we could stay in bed all day? Do we leave the office with energy to spare and plunge into a game of racquetball, or a jog, or an aerobics class? Or, do we wish we could have left after lunch and slouched into our living room easy chair for the remainder of the day?

There's no question that what we eat affects how we feel. And many of us are becoming so nutritionally savvy and concerned with our health that we have consciously tried to manipulate our diets to give us as much energy as possible. Adding tofu to your diet can be considered a wise choice, indeed. Tofu has been called a "protein powerhouse." In short, tofu enthusiasts get almost all of the benefits of animal protein, without any of its unhealthy effects.

A PROTEIN POWERHOUSE

The quality of all protein sources is measured by the presence of the eight essential amino acids that the body cannot synthesize. In tofu, you have found a vegetable-based food that contains all of these amino acids. And, tofu is a derivative of the soybean, one of the few legumes that has complete protein.

The protein from soy is nearly as good as milk protein when it comes to supporting the growth of laboratory animals. In fact, adult humans can provide for all of their protein requirements by eating soy as their only protein food. This is true despite the fact that two of the essential amino acids—methionine and cystine—are in shorter supply in soy foods than they are in other proteins.

So, how does tofu compete with beef and other popular protein staples? Sixty-five percent of the protein content of tofu is usable for tissue building. Nutritionists have measured beef at 67 percent Net Protein Utilization (NPU). That means that beef doesn't pack much more of a protein wallop when you take into consideration all of the saturated fat you ingest when you bite into it.

Although known as a "protein powerhouse," tofu, unlike beef and many other high-protein foods, is low in calories and saturated fats.

Chicken—which also has more fat than tofu—registers on the NPU index at the same exact spot as tofu. One gram of usable protein in tofu is accompanied by only 9 to 12 calories, which is significantly less than most animal-origin proteins.

If we take another 4-ounce slice of that cheddar cheese with which we earlier compared tofu and examine it in terms of getting more for our calories, we get even more good news about tofu and protein. This amount of cheese would have 28 grams of protein in its 451 calories—or 16 calories per gram of protein. The same amount of tofu might have only about 9 grams of protein, but only 9 calories per gram of protein.

The protein content of tofu may range from 5.5 percent in silken tofu to 10.6 percent in firm Chinese-style tofu. Regular soft tofu measures in at just under 8 percent. Eating 8 ounces of tofu can provide the same amount of usable protein as eating 3½ ounces of steak or 5½ ounces of ground beef. This same 8 ounces of tofu can provide an adult male with about 27 percent of his daily protein requirement.

A CALCIUM CHAMPION

If an adult male were to drink an 8-ounce glass of nonfat milk, he would receive only 20 percent of his Recommended Daily Allowance of protein. And, since milk and calcium are often spoken of together, you won't be surprised to learn that he would be getting 30 percent of his daily recommended calcium requirement. You may not know, though, that many types of tofu—unlike meat, poultry, and most fish—are excellent sources of calcium, as well.

Eight ounces of Nasoya tofu, as well as a number of other brands, have at least 20 percent of the Recommended Daily Allowance of calcium. With a growing emphasis on calcium, and with a fear of osteoporosis (the bone-degenerating disease that can affect calcium-deficient people), this should be welcome news to people who are trying to maintain a healthy diet.

Why do some types of tofu boast such significant amounts of calcium? In order to curdle tofu, it is often made with calcium-based coagulants. When this is done, the tofu contains even more of this important mineral than does the same amount of milk. It's important to note that the soybean itself contains more calcium than had previously been thought. If not properly prepared by the manufacturer, however, some of tofu's calcium is disposed of along with the whey.

Calcium sulfate, a naturally mined earth mineral, is used when making silken, soft, and firm styles of tofu. If calcium sulfate is listed on the label of your favorite brand of tofu, you know that its inclusion has significantly boosted the amount of calcium in the product. Sulfates are not to be confused with sulfites, which are preservatives often found on salad bars and known to cause allergies and other reactions.

If natural calcium chloride has been used as a coagulant for your tofu, you will also get big results in the calcium department. Tofu made with calcium chloride contains 23 percent more calcium than dairy milk of the same weight.

A PURE AND NATURAL FOOD

Clearly, more and more people are concerned these days not only with how the food they buy tastes, but also with how it was made and where it came from. Most of us can no longer ignore the warnings we hear about the pesticides, chemicals, or possible cancer-causing artificial ingredients that are in a great deal of our food supply.

This is reflected by the amount of health foods—now available not only in health food stores, but in many supermarkets as well—that are being consumed. Health food sales went from just $170 million in 1970 to $2 billion in 1981. According to the July 1989 issue of *Natural Foods Merchandiser*, health food sales totalled $3.5 billion in 1988, showing a solid 10 percent increase over 1987. And, in their June 1990 issue, *Natural Foods Merchandiser* reported 1989 sales of $3.9 billion—with an increase of more than 11 percent over the previous year!

A few decades ago, tofu could be bought only from large vats in health food stores. Now, in response to growing health food sales, packaged tofu is also available in most supermarkets nationwide. However, in contrast to many other foods, tofu is one product that has survived its introduction to supermarkets and still remains an absolutely natural food.

FREEDOM FROM CHEMICALS

At Nasoya, tofu has been made organically (with organic, stone-ground soybeans) and with only pure well water for more than ten years. Just what does it mean when a store-bought food product—or a soybean, for that matter—declares that it is organic? Although certifying procedures vary somewhat from state to state and country to country, "organic" generally means that no pesticides, chemicals, synthetically derived fertilizers, or fungicides have been used to grow the food.

Foods cannot become organic overnight, or in the course of one crop. A field must be declared chemical-free first. One of the nation's largest organic action certifying groups (there is a total of forty in the United States), the Organic Crop Improvement Association in Nebraska, says that a field can be certified organic only if a harvest occurs at least three years after the most recent use of unacceptable chemicals.

Hearty soybean plants thrive without the use of harmful pesticides, fungicides, or chemicals.

In addition to tofu's containing only natural ingredients, the curdling agents and solidifiers are natural. And, because tofu is a vegetable product, and is therefore low on the food chain, it naturally has less toxins than foods higher on the food chain.

Animal and dairy products are high on the food chain. And, for the most part, they can be relatively high in chemical toxins. These include pesticides, chemicals, and fertilizer residues, as well as the residues from the antibiotics and medications that the animals were given. These residues tend to accumulate in the fatty tissues of animals. Meat, poultry, and fish can contain up to twenty times more pesticide residues than legumes. Dairy products can contain up to five times more. However, since crops like soybeans are at the very base of the food chain and must be consumed by the farm animals, even if they're not organically grown, crop spraying is stringently controlled by the government.

Rest assured, though, that regardless of where the soybeans that your favorite tofu is made from were grown (and the United States is still the top world market for the crop), they have never been medicated or overdosed on drugs—like some animals—to get them to grow.

THE PURE WATER MAKES THE TOFU

Many of us are unhappily aware of the impurities in most of our municipal water systems. That's why bottled-water and delivered-water sales have increased dramatically. Most traditional tofu makers agree that good, clean water is an essential ingredient in making quality tofu. Since tofu is at least 80 percent water, it is impossible to make excellent tofu from poor-quality water. It is for this reason that in Japan, when a new tofu shop is considering a site for its plant, the quality of the water is the first thing that's considered.

City water is generally treated with chlorine and other chemicals to prevent bacterial contamination. Nasoya, however, like a number of the country's other environmentally and health-concerned companies, has found a way to keep the water pure. Rather than treating the water with chemicals, Nasoya has installed an ultraviolet light and mechanical filtration system to prevent any contamination from reaching the water. In addition, the water Nasoya uses comes from its own wells.

Part of the reason for using a system like Nasoya's is that tofu made with most municipally-treated water simply doesn't taste good. Think about it. You know that the wrong water can ruin a cup of coffee. Considering tofu's subtly sweet flavor, anything but the best-quality water is likely to be detected in off flavors in the finished product. There's no hiding anything in tofu.

IS THERE AN OCCASIONAL WHEEZE WHEN YOU EAT?

Millions of people suffer from food allergies. Some of these are hidden allergies, and the sufferer isn't even aware of them. Wheezing, coughing, stomach problems, and common colds often stem from food allergies. One of the most common allergies or food intolerances is to dairy products and milk. A person who cannot tolerate milk suffers from lactose intolerance. For years, many lactose intolerant people have known that soy could help replace milk in their diet, and have subsequently turned to soy milk products.

Similarly, tofu-based products and beverages can help those suffering from dairy allergies or lactose intolerance supplement their diet. You probably cannot imagine lasagna without cheese. Fortunately, a creamy tofu mixture—lower in fat than the cheese it replaces—can be used instead. How can a shake be enjoyed without milk? It simply needs to be whipped up with tofu.

If you are allergic to eggs, there are some great tofu alternatives. Scrambled tofu (see recipes) often cannot be differentiated from scrambled eggs. Similarly, quiches, breads, cakes, and cookies can also be made using tofu instead of eggs.

The perfect dairy substitute, tofu is a delicious alternative to eggs and cheese.

MORE GOOD NEWS

Basically, all the news is good when it comes to tofu and your health. For example, in addition to all of tofu's other nutritional benefits, it is also low in sodium. This is great news for those who need to be on a low-sodium diet because of high blood pressure. Those of us who want to help prevent the disease should consider this fact, also. Excess sodium is the second major risk factor in heart disease, the country's number one killer.

Tofu averages just 2 to 14 milligrams of sodium per 100 grams. Cottage cheese, by contrast, has about 256 milligrams of sodium. In addition, tofu is an excellent source of iron, a mineral in which many people, especially women, are deficient. Depending on the type of tofu (firmer styles have more iron), the United States Recommended Daily Allowance of iron in a 4-ounce serving of tofu can range between 10 percent and 20 percent. Tofu is full of other vitamins and minerals, too. One serving has 20 percent of the daily requirement of phosphorus. Tofu has a good supply of the important B vitamins, and of potassium. Eating tofu will also supply you with sufficient amounts of choline and fat-soluble vitamin E. Significant amounts of niacin, riboflavin, and thiamine are also present.

And, if you or someone you know has trouble digesting certain foods, you'll be happy to know that tofu is extremely digestible. In fact, it has a 95 percent digestibility rate (whole soybeans are just 65 percent digestible), making it perfect for those who wish to eat light foods that won't slow them down, and a great food choice for all age groups.

As we've mentioned, tofu can add a lot of versatility to the diets of those who are allergic to dairy products or eggs. And, finally, for those who must follow medically restricted diets for such conditions as diabetes, hypoglycemia, or heart disease, tofu can be a wonderful and tasty alternative to foods high in fat.

Cholesterol fighter. Fat attacker. Calcium champion. Tofu has indeed earned its reputation as a nutritional wonder food.

Tofu has been proving its extraordinary nutritional competence for over two thousand years. In ancient China, the people knew that tofu filled their need for nourishment during a period when other foods were not widely available. In the fourteenth century, Japanese peasants knew they were getting the same nutritional benefits as their emperors, as tofu became a favorite meal of all classes. Chinese immigrants in turn-of-the-century America owed much of their strength in building the country's railroads to the protein, vitamins, and minerals present in their daily intake of tofu. And, as most of us engage in the 1990s battle against cholesterol, we've realized that tofu is perhaps our very best nutritional friend.

The Vision

The clear blue September sky seemed to reach out towards infinity above the Concord, Massachusetts, fields. Brilliant white clouds, sparkling in the sun like opaque jewels, slowly drifted eastward toward the sea. As the prevailing westerlies dropped to earth, they swept across the maturing fields, bending the ripening stalks in flowing patterns, as though in anticipation of the ocean waves twenty miles away. Quietly I sat, mesmerized by this repetitive motion, until I began to notice, off in the distance, a farmer preparing to harvest his fields.

The farmer's dark tractor moved like a giant insect across the open fields. Slowly, I began to recognize this as the same machine that earlier in the year had come to spray the fields with a fine chemical mist—a mist that had drifted over the stone wall and settled, with an unpleasant odor, in my front yard. I had watched his machine before, spraying the fields during the spring and summer; his tractor had moved from row to row, the high-pitched whine of the chemical duster drowning out the quiet of the twilight hours. His fields grew quickly and appeared healthy, but I rarely ate his corn. Inevitably, I would remember the acrid smell of the herbicides, and my appetite would all but disappear.

A few miles away, on the other side of the Concord River, was Hutchin's Organic Farm. It was one of the most beautiful farms in New England, with rolling green fields sloping down to the river. People would come from all over to buy their produce. For many it had become a family outing, with station wagons and back seats stuffed with vegetables and children. Often, I would go there to buy my corn and talk with one of the brothers who ran the farm, discussing how people were slowly changing their eating habits to include more natural and organically grown foods. Over the years, I had been pleased to see the small shed adjacent to their farmhouse grow into a large roadside building to accommodate the increased demand for their fresh produce. It seemed that gradually, as the demand for organic vegetables grew, so did the demand for our tofu. America was changing, and a new wave of health consciousness was sweeping the country.

Today, there is no doubt that Americans are rapidly changing their diets to include fresher, higher-quality foods. A trip to the local supermarket reveals an incredible array of fresh fruits and vegetables, many of them organically grown. Twelve years ago, when we began marketing our products, the only organic food in the entire supermarket was our tofu. At that time, few people knew what the term "organic" meant, and even fewer knew what tofu was. The mere mention of tofu elicited many strange looks.

During our first year in business, I remember making deliveries for my driver, who was on vacation. When I got to the dock of one of the major chain stores to unload, I noticed a few of the receivers standing around watching me closely. I thought nothing of it until one of them came over and asked me if I ate tofu. I replied that I did, and he seemed surprised. Another remarked that he couldn't believe that I really ate tofu. "Are you sure?" he asked, raising an eyebrow as he continued to scrutinize me carefully. It was obvious that they had formed an opinion of what tofu eaters should look like, and I didn't fit the mold.

As I continued to unpack, the image of my driver flashed across my mind— long hair, an elfish face, strangely twinkling eyes, and a wild and woolly beard that eventually came to a jagged edge somewhere south of his chin. Finally, one of the men came up to me cautiously and said, "You look normal. But that other guy looks like he inhales the stuff." I almost fell off the dock laughing. I guess my mother was right all along. Those first impressions really do count.

We had quite a struggle trying to convince people to eat tofu during those first few years. Most people just weren't ready for vegetable protein foods back then. How could they have been? No one had told them that their bacon and eggs, cheeseburgers and fries, juicy steaks and rich desserts could end up blocking the blood flow to their hearts. Cholesterol and saturated fats weren't really an issue yet. At that time, shoppers were buying mostly meat and dairy products. Now, fresh produce, with its myriad shapes and colors, draws the most buyers. The American Heart Association and the American Cancer Society couldn't be happier with this trend. The meat and dairy industries, however, aren't so thrilled. Even with massive advertising campaigns and huge government subsidies, their sales continue to decline.

In many ways, I've come to believe that business is a forum for personal growth. It really tests our mettle. It proves our strengths and uncovers our weaknesses. It tempts us to compromise our principles. It is a hard taskmaster. In rare cases, businesses are founded with such strong and clear visions of the world they want to create that they take on a spirit all their own. Then, like a vacuum, this vision pulls the company ahead to success. "You don't have to be pushed," says Steve Jobs, founder of Apple Computer. "You run towards your vision of the world because it is so beautiful." Most businesses, however, end up succumbing to the tremendous pressures of the market, and become lost in the fog of conflicting demands. They lose their course and their original dream, with no compass to take them home. Their vision gets blurred, and they are often condemned to mediocrity. Great companies, like great countries, are guided by great guiding principles, which they do not compromise.

There have been a number of times at Nasoya when our basic principles came under heavy fire. I vividly remember the time when we almost threw in the towel on organic soybeans. We were in the middle of a price war with a local competitor. The price had fallen over two dollars a case on our basic tofu product, and the company was in trouble. As the war continued, a few of the people on the management team confronted me with the fact that we were wasting a great deal of money by continuing to buy organically grown soybeans. They wanted to switch immediately to a commercially grown variety to cut costs. They were right, looking at the situation solely from an economic point of view. There were other intangibles, I argued, but it was difficult for me to hang a price tag on them. The arguments continued for many weeks. I was caught in an almost impossible situation, having to choose whether the company's stated mission and my own personal beliefs were more important than the bottom line. No matter which way I turned, I hit a stone wall. Ultimately, we agreed to cut expenses and continue to manufacture an organic product, rather than to compromise our principles for a short-term gain. Fortunately for us all, the natural food markets and the supermarkets alike supported our decision. We were forced to tighten our belts. Yet, although everyone was affected, no one starved. We made sure of that. If anyone complained, we let them eat cakes—of tofu.

Today, as more people learn about tofu, we find that even the supermarket produce buyers are becoming convinced of its benefits. It wasn't long ago that only our natural foods buyers enjoyed tofu. Now, it's not surprising to find a young buyer from one of our major supermarket chains trying to cut down on his weight or his cholesterol, and asking us for a few tofu recipes. A few months ago, a group of us went back to that same supermarket chain where I had delivered tofu many years ago to make a presentation. We had prepared tofu and other foods to make a veritable feast for the buying department. We were not expecting a very large crowd, but, as it turned out, not only did the entire buying department come, some of the men from the receiving docks also joined us. I had to smile when one of them told us how he had been eating tofu regularly ever since one of our drivers had given him a recipe booklet on how to use it. Of course, his hair was quite long. And that beard. . . .

3. TOFU TIPS
A Shopper's Guide to Buying and Storing

J ust as there is whole, low-fat, and nonfat milk, there are also different types of tofu available for your use. And, just as you would refrigerate your dairy products as soon as you unpack them, there are simple ways to handle and store the packaged or fresh tofu you bring into your kitchen.

With about 70 million pounds of tofu being produced and eaten each year in the United States, many people are already adept at handling tofu. Millions of people are becoming just as familiar with draining a package of tofu as they are at cracking an egg or peeling an orange. And, even with the new high-tech advances in the packaging of some tofu—certain brands are now pasteurized or vacuum-packed—much of the care and handling of tofu, once it reaches your home, has gone virtually unchanged since it was first made over two thousand years ago.

TYPES OF TOFU

A few years back, tofu could be found only floating in vats in Oriental grocery or health food stores. But, today, tofu is found in colorful packages on the shelves of many supermarket chains. There are now two to four general types of tofu available. In addition, there are also a number of delicious specialty varieties that you might want to try.

The types of tofu you will probably see at your supermarket or health food store are extra firm, firm, soft, and silken. (Some stores may simply offer firm, medium, or soft.) Whether enjoying tofu straight from the package or using it as an ingredient in an exotic gourmet dish, there are important differences between the various types of tofu—differences that can make one more appropriate than another in a particular recipe or method of cooking.

The difference between firm tofu and soft tofu is solely related to the amount of water contained in the curd. Firm tofu is made by pressing the curds more than for a softer tofu, eliminating some of the water. Firm tofu is dense—from the compression of curds—and more solid than softer tofu. It would be more apt to stay together if it was stir-fried.

Firm and extra firm tofu provide more protein than the other types. Four ounces of extra firm tofu contain 16 grams of protein, whereas an equal serving of firm tofu contains 11 grams, soft contains 8 grams, and silken contains 6 grams.

Firmer tofu also contains more calories. A 4-ounce serving of extra firm contains about 120 calories, whereas a similar serving of firm might contain 100 calories; soft, 70 calories; and silken, 50.

Firm tofu (which resembles cheese, and can be sliced) is more like Chinese-style tofu. Softer tofu (which tends to have a custard- or cottage cheese-like consistency) is more like Japanese-style tofu.

Firm and extra firm tofu are perfect for stir-fry dishes, stews, and casseroles.

Firm tofu is probably the most common type of tofu in the United States. It holds its form well in recipes, but has a lighter consistency than the extra firm variety. Extra firm tofu is often used by cooks who want to stir-fry or pan-fry their tofu, and want to make sure that it holds its original shape—whether sliced or cubed—throughout the cooking and tossing process. Extra firm or firm tofu is a good choice in the preparation of stews or casseroles. When a recipe calls for tofu to be stuffed with a filling, firm-style tofu should be used.

Silken tofu is called *kinugoshi*, or *silken*, in Japan, and *tahu fah* in Southeast Asia. Generally, this tofu is not pressed during its production. Rather, the curds are allowed to set with the whey, leaving a creamy, soft product. It should be noted that although silken tofu is usually slightly softer than soft-style tofu, the terms are often used interchangeably, and one type can often be substituted for the other.

Soft and silken tofu can be blended into dips, dressings, puddings, parfaits, and sauces.

Soft and silken types of tofu are often used in preparing desserts like puddings and parfaits. They are also excellent cubed in soups and stirred into sauces. They blend well into dips and dressings, and are perfect whenever a creamy texture is desired, as in Hollandaise sauce. Soft tofu crumbles easily and can be used in place of ricotta or cottage cheese. Silken and soft tofu are popular in traditional Japanese cuisine.

If you have only soft tofu in your refrigerator, but want to prepare a meal that calls for firm tofu, don't despair. It's easy to turn soft tofu into firm tofu. A number of recipes call for firm, mashed tofu. If you don't have to worry whether the tofu retains its shape, simply put the soft tofu in a clean dish towel, and twist and squeeze it. Let it drain for a few minutes so that it loses moisture. Remove the tofu when it has the texture desired for your recipe.

Even if you need firm tofu that can be sliced or cubed, you can make it from fresh, soft tofu. First, the soft tofu should be wrapped in paper towels. It should then be pressed between two cutting boards or other flat object with a weight on top. After fifteen or twenty minutes, the water should have dripped out and you should have firm tofu. Lighter, shorter pressing keeps the tofu softer, whereas heavier, longer pressing results in firmer tofu.

This technique is handy for people who live in areas where only one type of tofu is available. They can vary the water content through pressing, and adjust the firmness to their cooking needs.

It is not possible, however, to turn firm tofu into soft tofu, since most of the water is already pressed out of firm tofu. If you do find yourself with only firm tofu on hand, and have a recipe that calls for soft tofu, you might want to throw the tofu in the blender with a few ounces of water. This will obviously give it a softer, creamier texture. You can also whip up your own tofu to meet your needs, as we'll show you in the next chapter.

If you're browsing through your health food store or supermarket for tofu, occasionally you may come across some interesting varieties in addition to the extra firm, firm, medium, soft, and silken styles. *Yaki-dofu*, for instance, is a type of Japanese tofu. If you see yaki-dofu, it will probably be cut into smaller pieces than other tofu. This kind of tofu has already been grilled over charcoal on both sides. Because of this, it is quite firm (often used in dishes like sukiyaki), and is often sold in cans. Yaki-dofu can also be prepared at home by grilling firm tofu.

Agé, sometimes referred to as *aburagé*, is tofu that has been deep-fried. Agé is hollow in the middle. It can be slit and stuffed with fillings. To prepare it, liquid is removed from firm tofu, and the tofu is fried until its texture is crisp and its color is brown. *Nama-agé* and *atsu-agé* are deep-fried like agé, but are made from a thicker cut of tofu. *Koya-dofu* is freeze-dried tofu. Koya-dofu is available in airtight packages, and must be reconstituted. This type of tofu absorbs the flavors of the liquid it is cooked or served with like a sponge, and has a very chewy texture.

Yuba is a Japanese delicacy made from the skin that forms on the surface of soy milk when it is heated uncovered. Although it is not tofu, because of its similar taste and history, it is often used in similar dishes. It is difficult to find, and is usually sold in sticks or rolls. You may come across it while shopping for tofu. If prepared properly (or if you're lucky enough to find a Buddhist Chinese vegetarian restaurant that serves yuba), you'll find that it has the texture and taste of meat.

SHOPPING FOR TOFU

In Southeast Asia, warm silken tofu, with tempting toppings, is sold by many street vendors to hungry passersby. In the West, however, we usually have to settle for the street-corner hot dog or pretzel.

Shopping for tofu in America may not be as easy as grabbing a hot dog, but with the tremendous growth in the soy and tofu industries, tofu has become much easier to find. Once available only to American consumers in Oriental markets, and then solely in health food stores, tofu is now available prepackaged in many health food stores and supermarket chains nationwide. It can also be found as an ingredient in many prepackaged convenience foods. There are frozen dinner entrées containing tofu, as well as tofu "hot dogs" and "candy bars."

Of course, tofu can still be purchased in Oriental markets or in bulk quantities in many natural food stores. When buying from these outlets, most experts stress the importance of finding out where the store gets its tofu, and how often the tofu is delivered. Because bulk tofu is not pasteurized, and is, therefore, more prone to contamination, it should not be more than a few days old. When buying tofu in bulk, you must also trust that the store is familiar with the handling of fresh tofu, and is aware that its water must be changed frequently.

Fortunately, tofu is one of the most economical protein sources we can buy. It can replace meat in many dishes, yet it usually costs much less. Frequently, tofu is sold in one-pound packages, but there are also 14-ounce, 10.5-ounce, 6-ounce, and many other quantities. When measuring tofu for recipes, a pound of tofu is equal to 2 cups. Many cooks use the water displacement method of measurement. To end up with a half-pound of tofu, for example, a 4-cup measuring cup should be filled to the 3-cup level with water. Then tofu should be added to bring the water up to the 4-cup mark. After some practice, estimates can easily be made.

Although we may enjoy making healthy and hearty meals for ourselves or our families, most of us are busy. In recent years, the rise in the buying of convenient packaged foods has been unprecedented. We work. We drive. We jog. We want to spend quality time with our children. In essence, we don't have much time to spare.

Fortunately, tofu—like many other foods—comes prepackaged. Within fifteen minutes, you can sauté your tofu with vegetables and have a hot, fresh meal. And, this meal will be 100 percent natural, with no additives or preservatives.

When shopping for tofu, "freshness" must be the key word. Think of a packaged tofu product as you would a dairy product. Most packaged tofu products will have a date stamp—as milk products do. Do not buy tofu after this date, and be very cautious if there is no date. We suggest that all refrigerated tofu products have clearly marked expiration dates.

Fresh tofu smells slightly sweet, and has a hint of a vegetable aroma. Tofu should not smell sour when you buy it. Just as you would not accept a milk product that smelled sour the day you brought it home from the market, you should not accept tofu bought in that condition. (Although, once you have bought fresh tofu and kept it for a few days, and it begins to smell slightly sour, there are ways to refreshen it, which we will describe shortly.) The tofu that you bring home should not feel slippery or have a pink or green tinge. This means it has begun to spoil.

To insure freshness, try to buy tofu that has at least a week left on its date code. This will allow you a few days to fit it into your meal-planning schedule. If you ever notice that a tofu package is swollen, do not buy it. This is usually a sign that the product has spoiled. Obviously, if you get tofu home and it shows any signs of mold or has a greenish color, you should return or discard it.

When purchasing tofu, keep in mind that it is perishable. Unless tofu is brick-packed—with an extended shelf life of nine months and no refrigeration necessary—it should be kept in a refrigerated section of your grocery store. Some grocers mistakenly think tofu is like a vegetable and does not need refrigeration. If you notice this situation in your market, you may want to inform a clerk or manager.

Don't assume that any tofu in the produce section is fresh unless it is cool to the touch. We've been to large chain markets and have seen fresh meat products on the shelves past their expiration date. And we've seen sushi (raw Oriental fish)—which must be refrigerated—stacked, unrefrigerated, in the produce section of a major market. This provides an ideal environment for the growth of harmful bacteria, and puts unknowing shoppers at a disadvantage. Sushi and tofu are just a few of the "new" foods in your supermarket with which clerks may not yet be fully familiar. If you suspect that the tofu is not being properly refrigerated, don't hesitate to let your grocer know.

In many markets, tofu is really branching out. It's not just in the dairy section or its own refrigerated department. It is also mixed

"Freshness" is the key word when shopping for tofu. Check the date stamp, and make sure that the tofu has been properly refrigerated.

and blended into other products. Ice Bean, Tofutti, Tofu-Lite, and other ice cream-like products use tofu as a base. There are fresh and frozen tofu hot dogs. Legume, Amy's Kitchen, and other manufacturers have put tofu in pot pies, lasagna, and other frozen dinners. Nasoya and others have made shelf-stable products—products that need no refrigeration—with a tofu base. There's Nayonaise, Nasoya's cholesterol-free tofu mayonnaise alternative product, and a line of Vegi-dressings. In other words, we can't tell you where in your supermarket you'll be most likely to find tofu. But, with the growth in tofu products overall, it seems to be difficult to find an aisle that *doesn't* have tofu or a tofu-based product lining its shelves.

STORING TOFU

When you get your frozen tofu lasagna or pot pie home, simply deposit it in your freezer until it's time to pop it into your microwave or conventional oven. More and more people, though, are also bringing home fresh or packaged tofu. And, although tofu is becoming a player in high-tech food manufacturing, much of its care once it reaches your home has changed little in the two thousand years since tofu was first made.

To keep your tofu at its freshest, store it in the refrigerator submerged in water, and change the water daily.

If you buy tofu that is packaged in water, just keep it in the refrigerator until you are ready to use it (remember to check the expiration date). Many quality brands of tofu—like Nasoya—are pasteurized. If, however, you know that tofu has not been pasteurized, you should drain the water and rinse the tofu. Then, cover the tofu with water, leaving it in either its original container or another bowl.

If you have opened prepackaged, pasteurized tofu, but you have not used it completely, place unused portions in a container of water in the refrigerator. It can be left in its own container or in one of your own. You may want to cover the tofu to prevent anything from falling into it and to keep it from absorbing the odors of other foods.

Since some packages are small, and tofu keeps best when surrounded by a lot of water, it may be helpful to transfer the tofu that you're refrigerating to a larger covered bowl or pan that contains up to a few quarts of water. The water should be changed frequently—daily, or every other day. Storing tofu in water can help it maintain its bulk and form. Although its texture and taste may begin to change, tofu can be kept for about a week to ten days in this manner.

Deep-fried tofu should not be stored under water. It should be refrigerated in an airtight container. Brick-pack tofu can be kept on a pantry shelf, but once it is opened it should be drained and kept under water in the refrigerator. The water should be changed daily.

When older tofu is being used, it works best in recipes where it takes on the flavors of a sauce or spice. A taco filling would be a good choice. Only the freshest tofu should be used for desserts or dips, or in a recipe that requires no cooking.

If you know in advance that you are not going to use the tofu you are buying for some time, or if you find it on sale and want to stock up, you can simply freeze it. If it is stored in water, slit the package and drain the water. Rinse the tofu, wrap it in plastic or freezer wrap, and freeze it immediately.

Tofu freezes beautifully! Simply drain the tofu, rinse it, wrap it, and pop it into the freezer. It will stay fresh for up to five months.

Freezing will change the texture of the tofu. It will become chewy and spongelike. It may also appear to be a creamy beige color. But, in this form, many people find tofu to be an excellent meat replacement in such dishes as chili or pot pies. It takes on the texture of ground beef, and is also a good addition to sauces or casseroles. Although it cannot be frozen indefinitely, tofu can remain fresh in the freezer for up to five months.

While most tofu aficionados throw out tofu as soon as it begins to get sour, there are other alternatives. If your refrigerated tofu begins to smell slightly sour, you can drain it and freeze it. Freezing tofu in a plastic bag—after you have drained it and pressed all the excess air out—works well. Freezing tends to revive tofu. Before using it again, make sure to thaw it completely.

Frying tofu that is beginning to go sour can also mask the flavor. In addition, if tofu has been in the refrigerator a few days, and you would like to extend its life, you can boil it to kill any bacteria that may have developed. Boil the tofu in about two inches of water to which a pinch of salt has been added, and then let it simmer for five to ten minutes. The tofu will become light, puffy, and moist, and can be used as though it were fresh.

If not used right away, the tofu should be drained, rinsed in cold water, and stored in the refrigerator under water. Salt, in addition to increasing tofu's life span, can prevent it from becoming hard when cooked. However, because boiling tends to give tofu a harder, chewier texture, and also changes tofu's flavor a bit, it should be used only when needed.

There are not many foods—animal or vegetable—that seem to have as many lives as tofu. So keep a supply on hand, and store it with care. Once you get into the tofu habit, you'll be surprised by the number of delicious, healthful dishes that can be made with this wonderfully versatile food.

4. DO-IT-YOURSELF TOFU
Making Tofu at Home

T he scent of bread baking in an oven, or the smile of a child who has just stolen the last drops of homemade cake frosting from a mixing bowl, make the baking of bread or a special cake even more special.

There's no doubt that most people are busier today than ever. Convenience foods permeate the marketplace. Tofu is no exception. It comes conveniently packaged and ready to eat in supermarkets all over the country. But, occasionally, many of us enjoy rolling up our sleeves and preparing homemade delicacies.

It may come as a surprise to some that whipping up a batch of tofu is no more difficult than baking a loaf of bread or preparing a cake. For some families, making yogurt, ice cream, wine, or cheese at home can be an adventure. Preparing tofu is a similar adventure, and is much like making cheese.

We are buying more packaged convenience food items than ever before. But, at the same time, there is a growing interest in fresh and natural homemade foods. More natural food cookbooks are being bought now than ever before.

The weekend chef is a new phenomenon. Busy career couples—who have little time to cook during the week—often prepare nutritious, hearty meals on the weekend and freeze or refrigerate the bounty for the week ahead. Pots of vegetarian stew and cauldrons of vegetable soup are popular choices. But what about tofu?

Plenty of tofu aficionados have discovered how to prepare their own fresh tofu, whether it's for a leisurely lunch or in preparation

Like baking bread, tofu making can be an adventure shared by the entire family. And your homemade tofu may be the best you've ever tasted!

for a whole week of delicious meals. We'll give you a step-by-step guide for preparing one pound of fresh tofu. And, you can alter this recipe to fit your own specific needs.

WHAT YOU'LL NEED: EQUIPMENT AND INGREDIENTS

You won't need any out-of-the-ordinary or exotic equipment to make tofu. Most of the tools may be found right in your own kitchen. Here's a checklist:

- A deep container that will hold 4 cups of water and 1 cup of dried soybeans overnight.
- An electric blender. (A food processor, grain or food mill, meat grinder, or juice machine may be substituted.)
- A heavy-bottom 4-quart pot.
- A 4-quart saucepan.
- 2 colanders.
- Cheesecloth. Enough cheesecloth should be available to line the bottom of one colander and to be wrapped four times around one pound of tofu.
- 3 large bowls.
- A flat object weighing 3 to 5 pounds. This could be a water-filled jar or a can of food.
- Candy thermometer (optional).

Many health food stores feature tofu-making kits that include some of the equipment and ingredients you'll need. But, we'll show you how to make tofu on your own, without having to purchase a kit.

Tofu making requires only three ingredients: soybeans, a solidifier, and pure spring water.

Just as there is not much equipment required to make tofu, and that equipment is easy to find, you will need only a few ingredients to follow in the centuries-old tradition of making homemade tofu. To make one pound of fresh tofu, you will need:

- 1 cup dried soybeans (descriptions of different types of soybeans follow).
- Water (preferably pure spring water).
- 2¼ teaspoons Epsom salts dissolved in 1 cup water.

We've already talked about how economical it is to purchase high-protein, low-fat packaged tofu when you compare it with the price of beef or chicken. When you take the plunge and begin making your own tofu, you'll save even more money. Most tofu can be made at home for virtually pennies a serving. That's because soybeans, like most legumes, are reasonably priced. At Nasoya, organic soybeans—soybeans grown without chemicals or pesticides—are used, and many home chefs also prefer them. You might want to check with your local health food store or farmer's market to see if it carries organic soybeans. They are also available through the many mail-order food companies around the country. (See the mail-order list on page 165.)

Whether or not you decide to use organic soybeans, look for large, seeded soybeans, rather than small ones. The larger the bean, the less okara—a by-product of tofu making that we'll describe later—remaining, and the more tofu you'll have.

Nasoya uses Hilum soybeans, which sport a clear spot on the surface. These are generally thought to be of better quality for tofu making than beans that have a black, rather than clear, spot. The spot usually appears on the center, or head, of the bean.

There are over three hundred varieties of soybeans available. The United States used to produce mainly Oriental-type soybeans. These are higher in protein content than they are in oil. However, because of the increasing demand for soybean oil in recent years, the country began growing mainly beans that are high in oil. This type, however, is *not* best for making tofu. Hilum, as we mentioned,

Organically grown soybeans ready to be made into tofu.

or Vinton variety soybeans are the best choices for tofu making. If you have any questions, ask a salesperson at your local market which of the three hundred varieties of soybeans they carry.

In order to reap one pound of fresh tofu, start with one cup of dried soybeans. However, one pound of tofu is only a medium-sized cake, so if you need to make more, just increase the amount of beans and Epsom salts used. Two cups of dried soybeans would create two pounds of tofu, and so forth.

The recipe also calls for 2¼ teaspoons of Epsom salts. This will be used as your solidifier. In other words, it acts as the curdling agent for the tofu. Epsom salts are used in place of rennet, which curdles cow's milk, but will not curdle soy milk.

Epsom salts, or magnesium sulfate, are found in supermarkets and drugstores, and are quite inexpensive. They are not to be confused with sulfites, which are used as anti-browning agents in foods and salad bars, and cause allergic reactions in many people. Generally, Epsom salts are used as a laxative (although the small amount in tofu does not have that effect), or to bathe or soak feet. Using Epsom salts in tofu making results in light, sweet tofu.

Although we recommend using Epsom salts—because of their wide availability, reasonable price, and ability to produce sweet tofu—it is also possible to use nigari, a natural solidifier that comes from sea salt; lemon or lime juice; vinegar; or calcium sulfate. Until recent years, most nigari, or magnesium chloride, came from the Sea of Japan. It is used in many commercial brands of tofu and is available in most health food stores and Japanese markets. It is usually more expensive than Epsom salts. Calcium sulfate, another commercially used solidifier, has the advantage of adding more calcium to the resulting tofu.

Both Epsom salts and nigari make sweet and light tofu. If lemon or lime juice or distilled vinegar is used as the solidifier, you will taste it in the finished product. They make the tofu taste a bit sour. Calcium sulfate, also known as gypsum, makes light, sweet, velvety tofu. Unfortunately, it is often difficult to find in local stores.

When making tofu at home, pure spring water will yield the best and sweetest results.

When speaking of how your homemade tofu will taste, it is important to mention the type of water that you'll use. As we discussed previously, since water is a primary ingredient of tofu, it often determines the taste of the tofu. It is possible to simply use tap water to prepare tofu. However, because of the impurities found in many water systems, we would not recommend this as the ideal choice. Distilled water is also not recommended, since the distillation process removes all of the water's natural minerals. Instead, pure spring water should be used to produce the best-tasting tofu.

So, in the process of making tofu, there are only three ingredients: soybeans, a solidifier, and pure water. That's all you need.

WHAT'S IT ALL ABOUT?

Tofu making begins with the cooking of finely ground or puréed soybeans in water to produce soy milk. Then, the soybean hulls are removed, resulting in a steaming hot soy milk. Next, the soy milk is reheated, the solidifier is added, and curds and whey are produced. Lastly, the curds are pressed to form cubes.

After we go through the specific steps involved in making tofu, we'll tell you about the many interesting and nutritious uses there are for the whey and other "leftovers" of the tofu-making process.

STEP ONE: MAKING THE SOY MILK

Much as cheese comes from cow's milk, soy milk is the foundation for tofu. Soy milk has no cholesterol, but, compared with dairy milk, it is also low in calcium.

The soy milk you will make at home may be the freshest and sweetest you've ever tasted. You may want to set aside a few glasses for drinking before you continue making your tofu. Since much store-bought soy milk includes added ingredients like oils or sweeteners, it is definitely not recommended for use when you make your own tofu.

Most of the steps involved in making tofu encompass preparing the soy milk. First, soak soybeans in 4 cups of water overnight. This should be done in a container large enough so that the beans are covered to allow for expansion. The beans will expand to about two and a half times their dry size.

The soybeans should not be left soaking for longer than 15 hours. If you notice the beans sprouting or the water becoming foamy, you've let the beans soak too long.

Drain the beans once they have soaked overnight. Then, purée the beans in batches in a blender, using 1 cup of beans to 1½ cups of water at a time, and processing each batch for 2 minutes. Next, take another 5 cups of water and combine it with the puréed beans (known in traditional Japanese tofu-making language as *gô* purée) in a heavy-bottom 4-quart saucepan. You may wish to coat the pot with non-stick oil or spray so that the beans will be less likely to burn or stick to the bottom.

Bring the mixture in the pot to a slow boil, stirring frequently to avoid sticking. When it has boiled to the point that foam has begun to rise, lower the temperature and simmer the mixture for 10 to 15 minutes. (At this point, the traditional Japanese tofu masters referred to the soy product simply as *gô*.) This heating time is necessary to

1. Soak 1 cup of dried soybeans overnight in a large bowl containing 4 cups of water. The soybeans should not be left soaking longer than 15 hours. If the water becomes foamy or the beans sprout, the beans have soaked too long.

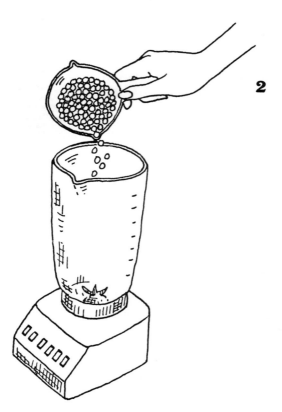

2. Once the beans have soaked overnight, drain off the water. Then, using a blender or food processor, purée the drained beans in batches, adding 1½ cups of water to each cup of beans. Process each batch for about 2 minutes.

3. In a 4-quart saucepan, stir together the puréed beans and 5 cups of water, bringing the mixture to a boil. Lower the heat, and simmer the mixture for 10 to 15 minutes.

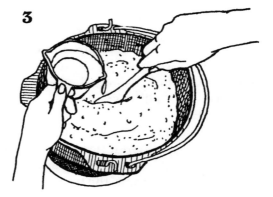

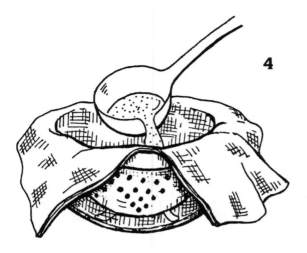

4. Ladle the mixture, now called gô, into a cheesecloth-lined colander that has been set over a bowl. Strain out the liquid into the bowl. Because the liquid will be hot, you may want to do this in the sink. Strain out as much of the liquid as possible.

5. Place the cheesecloth-wrapped residue—a fiber-rich product called okara—in a bowl of cold water, and move the cheesecloth back and forth through the water. This will help you extract additional soy milk from the okara.

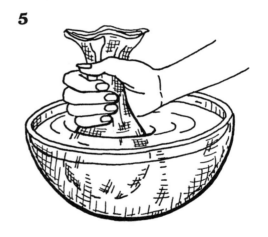

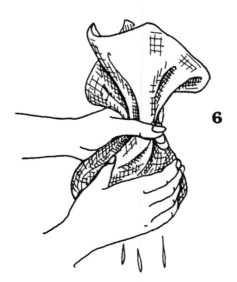

6. Place the cheesecloth-wrapped okara back in the colander, pour 2 cups of water through the okara, and press, squeeze, and twist the cloth to drain the water into the bowl. What remains in the bowl is soy milk—possibly the sweetest soy milk you've ever tasted!

destroy substances in soybeans called *trypsin inhibitors*, which prevent the body from absorbing protein.

Next, ladle the gô into a colander that has been lined with cheesecloth, and place the colander on top of a large bowl that will catch the liquid. You may want to do this in the sink, since the liquid will be hot. Strain out as much of the soy milk as you can. The residue—grounds, called okara—will remain in the cheesecloth. Okara is a fiber-rich product with many uses, which will later be discussed in detail.

Lift the cheesecloth out of the colander and place the wrapped okara in a large bowl of cold water. Stir the water through the okara in the cheesecloth. Next, place the cheesecloth-wrapped okara back in the colander, and again strain the liquid into the bowl. Pour 2 cups of water through the okara, again straining this through the cloth. Don't be hesitant. Press it, squeeze it, and twist it to drain all of the water into the bowl. What remains in your bowl is soy milk. It's appropriate for drinking, cooking—or making tofu!

> Your homemade soy milk will be fresh, sweet, and free of additives. If you like, set aside a few glasses for drinking!

STEP TWO: MAKING TOFU FROM SOY MILK

Now that you have begun making your own tofu, you've become part of a two-thousand-year-old tradition. You took dried soybeans and made your own milk. Basically, all that's left to do is curdle the milk and form your creation.

Pour the soy milk you've made into a 4-quart saucepan and heat to 180°F, or just below the boiling point. Add a third of the Epsom salts solution to the soy milk. Stir well. Wait for the milk to settle, sprinkle another third of the solution over it, and stir gently. Let this mixture sit covered for about 8 minutes. Next, sprinkle the last third of the Epsom salts solution over the milk, cover, and let sit for about 4 minutes. You'll begin to see the curdled milk gather together into soft curds. While this is happening, gently stir the top 2 to 4 inches of the mixture. You'll see a clear yellow liquid appearing between the curds. This is the whey.

Line a colander with a quadruple layer of cheesecloth. Place the colander over a large bowl, and ladle the curds and whey into the cheesecloth. Be careful not to break up the curds. The whey will drain out through the cheesecloth, and the curds will remain. The whey can be saved for other uses that we'll describe later.

Fold the cheesecloth over the top of the drained curds and put a flat weight (such as a water-filled jar or a food can) on top of the wrapped curds. The weight should be distributed as evenly as possible over the wrapped curds. Whey will continue to drip out through the cheesecloth, while the curds will solidify into a block of tofu. Keep in mind the type of tofu you'd like to end up with—firm or soft. The more whey that you allow to drip out, the firmer the resulting tofu will be. A usable block of tofu will result in 1½ to 2 hours. When the tofu is completely cooled, unwrap it, and—if you're not going to enjoy the fruits of your labor immediately—immerse it in cold water and store it in the refrigerator. It will stay fresh in the refrigerator for a week or so if kept in water. It doesn't have to be covered, but covering will prevent odors from permeating the tofu.

7

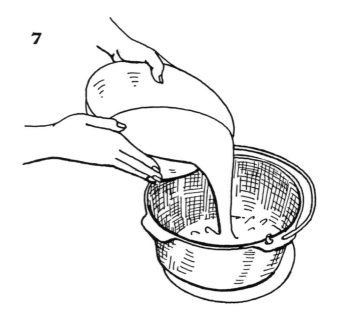

7. Pour the soy milk into a 4-quart saucepan, and heat to just below the boiling point (180°F). A candy thermometer will be helpful in determining the proper cooking time.

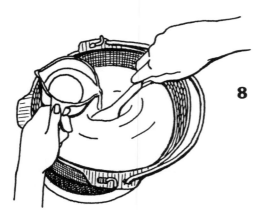

8

8. Mix the Epsom salts solution by dissolving 2½ teaspoons of Epsom salts in 1 cup of water. Add a third of the solution to the soy milk, and stir well. After the milk settles, stir in another third of the solution, and let the mixture rest for 8 minutes. Sprinkle the remaining solution into the mixture, cover, and let sit for 4 minutes.

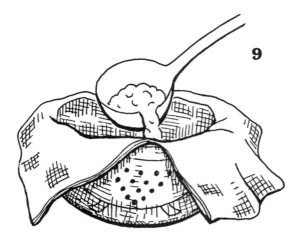

9

9. After the solution has formed curds and whey, ladle the mixture into a colander that has been lined with a quadruple layer of cheesecloth and set over a large bowl. The whey will drain out, and the curds will remain in the cloth.

10

10. Fold the cheesecloth over the top of the curds, and place a flat weight on top of the cheesecloth. Your tofu will be ready in 1½ to 2 hours.

   If your recipe calls for a perfect block of tofu, punch holes in a metal loaf pan with a hammer and nail, spacing the holes about ½-inch apart on the sides and bottom of the pan. Line the pan with cheesecloth, ladle in the curds, and cover with more cheesecloth. As a weight, use another loaf pan, filling it with water.

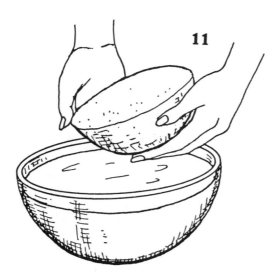

11

11. To store your finished tofu, remove it from the cheesecloth and immerse it in cold water. Place the bowl, covered, in the refrigerator—or enjoy your creation immediately!

SNAZZY WAYS TO CUT, DICE, OR CRUMBLE YOUR TOFU

If you've followed along, your tofu is virtually *handmade* homemade. So, if you'd like, take a handful and crumble it. Crumbled tofu is popular in dishes where it replaces scrambled eggs and in dishes like chili, where it replaces hamburger. For soups, use a spoon or melon baller to take scoops out of your tofu block. This creates tofu balls that can be dropped into your soup.

Some people like to make their tofu into what is called the chrysanthemum cut. To achieve this effect, cut your tofu cake into quarters. Place the tofu so that the largest surface is uppermost, and cut lengthwise and crosswise at intervals of about ¼ inch, being careful not to cut all the way through each quarter of the tofu. This can be decorative in a soup bowl or other similar dish. Simply open up the ends of each resulting piece. You can also leave your home-made tofu in large blocks for cooking, or dice or cut it into rectangles for snacking.

You may decide to transform a 1-pound block of your homemade—or store-bought—firm tofu into a completely different form. Here are some equivalent measurements that should come in handy when you're creating some of our recipes, or your own masterpieces. When 1 pound of tofu is made into 1-inch cubes, for example, it becomes equivalent to 2⅔ cups. If you crumble or mash your pound of tofu, it will equal 2 cups. When the tofu is pressed or squeezed, and then crumbled, it will equal 1¼ cups. If you purée the 1-pound block of tofu, you'll end up with 1¾ cups.

Crumble the tofu by squeezing it in your hand. This is great in scrambled tofu dishes, chili, and any other dish in which tofu is replacing ground beef.

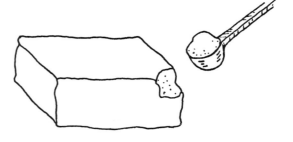

Use a spoon or melon baller to form tofu balls for soup.

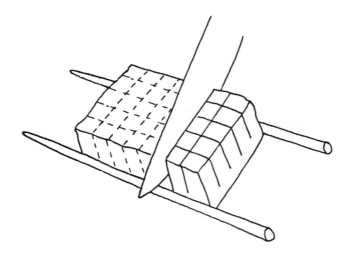

For the chrysanthemum cut, cut through the tofu lengthwise and crosswise at ¼-inch intervals, leaving the bottom ½ inch intact. To make sure that you don't slice all the way through, place the tofu between chopsticks. To finish the decoration, gently separate the ends.

Make lengthwise and crosswise cuts to form tofu cubes for shish kebab, stir-fry, and many other delicious dishes.

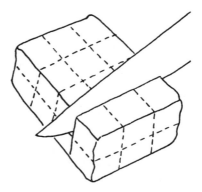

TURNING YOUR TOFU INTO AGÉ

Once you've succeeded in creating your own tofu, you might want to try a variation. You could, for instance, turn it into agé, the Japanese-style fried, stuffed tofu that we discussed in the last chapter.

To do this, cut a block of tofu into slices as large or small as you'd like for stuffing. To remove excess moisture, place the slices on a cloth, and place another cloth on top. Pat the tofu until it seems dry.

Choose an oil for frying. Remember that the flavor of the oil will be absorbed by the tofu. (See page 63 for a discussion of cooking oils.)

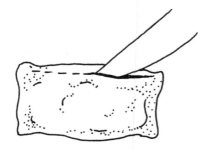

To make agé pouches, cut a thin slice from one end of the agé, or cut a slit up the side. Use your thumbs to separate the two layers.

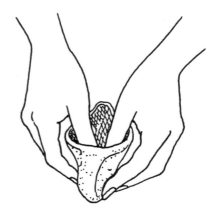

To make the agé, heat enough oil in a pot to cover your tofu slices. Drop in a piece of tofu. If the oil is hot enough, the tofu should fall to the bottom and then rise back to the top quickly. As soon as it rises, remove your agé from the pot, and let it cool on absorbent cloth or paper toweling. You can leave your agé as is, or, if you're concerned about excess oil, you may want to drop the slices into boiling water for a few minutes. Then rinse the agé in cold water and drain it.

To make a pouch for stuffing, simply use a rolling pin and go back and forth over each agé slice. This makes it easier to open. The top can be cut off, or a slit can be cut up the side.

WHERE THERE'S OKARA, THERE'S A WHEY

In today's world, many things are disposable. For instance, when you buy a frozen dinner, you throw out the tray, along with the carton it came in. As you've probably surmised, soybeans and the products that are derived from them are incredibly useful. There is virtually no waste. That's why soybeans have been for centuries—and promise to be in the future—an extremely important food source.

In preparing the soy milk that turned into your tofu, we mentioned okara as the grounds, or residue, of the milk after the first boiling. Okara is a good source of both protein and fiber.

Making tofu from scratch is one of the few ways to get okara. It is generally not available outside of the Far East. Sometimes it can be obtained from American tofu shops, but the freshest okara is a "leftover" of your tofu-making process.

Okara can be formed into patties and cooked as a hamburger replacement, or used as an extender in tofu burger dishes. Because it doesn't change the flavor or texture of food, it can also be added to baked goods, such as breads or muffins. You might also try it in pancakes, waffles, and pie crusts.

Some chefs prefer to wash okara before using it. To do this, place it in a sieve in a bowl of water. Stir it a bit, and then drain it in cheesecloth. Make sure all of the moisture drains out. If you feel you need finer okara, you can grind it or push it through a sieve.

Okara has definite substance. By looking at it, you'd probably guess it has various uses. However, when looking at the whey—the pale, yellow liquid you caught in your bowl while making tofu—you might not guess that it, too, has some interesting uses. The fact that there are uses for whey shows that there's absolutely no waste when it comes to cooking with soybeans.

Whey contains much of the solidifier you used when making your tofu. It also contains quite a bit of the bean's carbohydrates. You should be warned, however, that whey can be gaseous.

Many people find whey to be an excellent additive to yeast breads. It extends the effect of the yeast. Like okara, whey has protein, and also is high in the B vitamins. It's a tasty base for vegetables and soups, too. And, some people seem to really enjoy drinking whey straight, as a beverage. When Nasoya first began, the man who did the curdling had trouble starting his day without a mug of whey. In fact, he was so enamored of the whey that for months after he left for a new job, he would stop by the Nasoya plant in the morning for his swig of whey.

Believe it or not, your tofu making may also make you a better housekeeper. The whey from your tofu has been shown to be an excellent cleaner. You can begin by cleaning your tofu-making or other cooking equipment with it. This was frequently done at Nasoya when the business first started.

You can even clean your floors with whey. Because of the natural oils inherent in whey, you will add a special gleam to wood floors by using just a little elbow grease and some whey. That's another one of the many "wheys" tofu is beneficial.

Breaking Ground

"I was determined to know beans," Thoreau wrote in his journal as he sat reflecting on the garden that he had grown beside Walden Pond in Concord, Massachusetts. Attempting to unburden himself of the cares of his contemporaries, and to unlearn the ways of a too-complex world, Thoreau immersed himself in the silence and simplicity of a life of natural beauty and contemplation. Many a sequestered afternoon would find him sitting quietly by his cabin, enjoying the breeze blowing across the inlet of the pond, watching his garden grow.

Both Thoreau and his mentor, Emerson, believed in the perfection and harmony of nature, and in a reverence for all living things. Both men lived according to their philosophies, and their insights were captured in the writings and lectures they left behind. Thoreau continually preached the virtues of a simple life. He well understood the perils and desperation of too much complexity, and wrote of the necessity of going back to nature. In many ways, he was the herald of an age to come, when men would become lost in their machines, estranged from nature and themselves. "The majority of men live lives of quiet desperation," he observed.

We are part of the whole, and when we move away from what is natural, we diminish ourselves. When this happens, the circle of wholeness, which connects us to everything else, becomes broken. The saying, "We are what we eat," was based on this concept. How we treat our bodies every day, including what foods we choose to eat, has a profound effect on our lives.

This relationship between diet and health was well understood thousands of years ago. "Let food be thy medicine," stated Hippocrates, the father of modern medicine. Among modern-day cultures around the world, examples of longevity can still be found among the Hunzakut of Pakistan, the Vilcabamban of Ecuador, and the Abhasian of the Soviet Union. Common to all of these people is a diet rich in natural, organically grown foods, with only small amounts of animal foods, saturated fats, and cholesterol. In these traditional cultures, protein is derived primarily from vegetable sources, and diets consist mainly of whole grains, beans, vegetables, and fruits. These peoples have a wholeness and vibrancy—largely as a result of the foods they consume daily.

This return to a simple life and diet is what Thoreau wanted to achieve in his experiment on Walden Pond. Both Thoreau and Emerson understood the importance of eating simple, natural foods, and, as a result, became vegetarians. While Emerson wrote and lectured on the unity of all life, Thoreau sat by his cabin on the edge of Walden Pond tuning into his beans. It's a wonder he didn't discover tofu.

Growing up in the Concord area, I spent many days at Walden Pond. I had visited the site of Thoreau's cabin and had read his journals and books. In college, I studied Emerson's essays and his transcendentalist philosophy. I came to believe that all of nature is in some way unified, and that to be a whole person, you have to regain your original connection with nature. Over the years, I slowly gravitated towards eating a simple diet based on whole grains, beans, fruits, and vegetables.

I suppose it was only natural that something inside me would click when I first discovered tofu in a Chinese grocery. It was as if I had uncovered an age-old secret locked within the humble block of tofu, waiting to be given form. Here before me was what the Taoists refer to as the "uncarved block," a perfect form possessing unlimited potential. After becoming acquainted with the product, my partner Bob and I became quite convinced that this highly nutritious food from the Orient would soon be celebrated in America for its remarkable versatility. And we wanted to become part of the celebration.

We knew that many people were actively seeking foods that were lower in saturated fats and cholesterol. Too many were suffering unnecessarily from heart disease and other related illnesses, and the scientific community was slowly realizing that the standard American diet, rich in saturated fats and cholesterol, was the culprit. People were beginning to look for heart-healthy alternatives. This meant a diet that reduced dependence on meat and dairy products and centered more on quality vegetable proteins. Tofu was perfect for this. We felt that tofu had enormous potential for creating change in the American diet. If a half million Americans were suffering from heart disease every year, perhaps by altering their dietary habits and substituting tofu for the meat or cheese in some of their favorite dishes, they could live longer, healthier lives. As we learned more about tofu's high lecithin, linoleic acid, and polyunsaturate levels, we began to understand the key role that this remarkable protein food could play in America's change to heart-healthy eating.

Equally important to us was the fact that tofu was made from soybeans, one of the United States' most plentiful crops. It was our hope that tofu would become as American as apple pie. (I'll admit, we were optimists.) Even Henry Ford had gotten excited when he began to realize the soybean's incredible potential. In the 1930s, he had introduced the bean to American farmers, who were still suffering from the effects of the Great Depression. Having been raised on a farm himself, Ford was forever aware of the needs of the family farmer, and viewed the soybean as an answer to a prayer. He envisioned a time when the soybean would become one of America's most important crops. With this in mind, he began to create industrial uses for the bean in his automobile manufacturing process. There is a well-publicized photo of a man with an axe swinging full force at one of Ford's new car bumpers, which was made from soybean oil. As a tribute to Henry's ingenuity, the axe just bounced off.

Henry Ford was a practical man who knew the value of a simple diet. He kept himself fit by riding his bicycle daily and eating tofu regularly. Henry once hosted a dinner party where he introduced the press to his newly discovered "wonder" food. That night, he had prepared a complete meal from soy nuts to soy milk, including soy cheese (tofu) and desserts made from the soybean. The pièce de résistance was his arrival in a suit spun entirely from soybean fibers. Henry Ford, it seemed, was also determined to know beans.

Once we made the decision to manufacture tofu, we promised ourselves that whatever we made would be of the highest quality possible. This meant finding the right ingredients—organic soybeans, pure well water, natural calcium or magnesium earth, and sea mineral coagulants. The first step was to find a location that would provide us with the pure well water we needed. In the summer of 1976, Bob and I began looking in the Concord area, but moved progressively west after realizing that the price of property, rental or otherwise, was out of reach. By late summer, we had found what we felt was a suitable location, with excellent well water. It was an old dairy farm. The farm was equipped with a small dairy processing room that had been run until the early 1970s, when the demand for door-to-door milk deliveries declined.

The farm was a perfect starting location for us—except for one thing. The previous owner had never thrown one darn thing away. Strewn about the property were derelict trucks, tires, milk crates, and machinery parts to which the farmer had developed a sentimental attachment. It is nearly impossible to describe the frustration we went through trying to prepare the dairy for operation. We must have gone to the landfill with over fifty truckloads of artifacts that had accumulated on that farm over the years. I can still recall the farmer standing over us, red-faced and hollering, snatching as many of his possessions as he could from the truck as we tried in vain to load it up. This ritual was repeated day after day. And each time, we shook our heads in disbelief as we watched him angrily hauling his valued objects up the hill to his already cluttered farmhouse.

It took us nine frustratingly long months to finally get the tofu operation going. It was during the first week of April 1978 that our first tofu started coming off the production line. We began by making only bulk tofu, but it wasn't long before we introduced our packaged variety. Even we were surprised by the reception our tofu received. Almost immediately, we were inundated with orders for over three thousand pounds of tofu per week to be shipped to natural food customers from Maine to Philadelphia.

I suppose that what really surprised us was the demand for tofu from people looking for protein alternatives. And once people began using our product, they used it in everything from appetizers to desserts. Unfettered by tofu's traditional uses, Americans were throwing tofu into their ethnic melting pots and coming up with the most amazing discoveries. Weekly, we heard about a new tofu recipe someone had tried that had eliminated the fat and cholesterol from their favorite dishes. An example is the lasagna my grandmother baked, made lighter by the substitution of tofu for ricotta cheese. Or, the Greek salad that used marinated tofu instead of feta cheese. A recipe for tofu blintzes arrived. Someone told us about a stew in which they replaced the meat with tofu that had been marinated and fried. There were tofu quiches and Texas chilis. Even the Oriental dishes that used to be served with meat were now being made with tofu instead—like sweet and sour tofu, tofu teriyaki, and stir-fried tofu and vegetables. Someone even tried to substitute pressed tofu for turkey on Thanksgiving. At that point, we wondered whether we hadn't gone a little too far. We didn't want the Daughters of the American Revolution ganging up on us. Not yet, anyway.

In retrospect, the American spirit of adventure, as much as anything else, helped our little tofu shop grow to become the company that it is today. I suppose it was inevitable that we would become bored with our meat, potato, and white bread diets, especially those of us from the sixties generation. While I was growing up, we ate meat almost every day, and sometimes twice a day, whether we wanted to or not. It had become part of the American way. Luckily, things change. People are eating meatless meals several times a week now, and including more whole grains and fresh vegetables in their diets. They're looking for new ways of enjoying their lighter fare, and tofu seems to be fitting right in. I think Thoreau would have been pleased. If Henry Ford were around, he'd probably have built a tofu factory by now, and spun his car's upholstery from the leftover soybean hulls.

5. TEMPTING TOFU
The Art of Cooking With Tofu

Would you have to twist your child's arm to get him to dig into a slice of creamy cheesecake? How easy would it be to tempt him with a fluffy, blueberry syrup-topped pancake?

Would your husband be opposed to having a moist square of applesauce cake tucked into his briefcase, or a silken strawberry mousse whipped up after dinner?

Would you mind having crisp, hot waffles served to you in bed for breakfast, or coming home to fresh, steaming lasagna? Would you have to be asked twice to sample spicy shish kebab, creamy stroganoff, or festive chili? Probably not. These are mainstream dishes—popular and delicious.

Many people are surprised to learn that hundreds of comparable dishes can be made easily—and without alteration to their flavor—with tofu. Incorporating low-calorie, no-cholesterol, high-protein tofu into your diet can be as rewarding as enjoying a rich mousse or a mouth-watering pizza.

Tofu sold in your supermarket in white cakes can be sliced and eaten right from the package. Or, it can be marinated, stir-fried, or scrambled. Tofu is also a skilled magician. It can hide in your cannelloni, taco, or stew, and—before your eyes—take on the flavor of those and many other foods. As we'll describe later, you can take many of your favorite recipes, as well as those you'd like to try, and easily substitute tofu for beef, poultry, fish, cheese, or eggs.

You'll find it easy and fun to incorporate low-calorie, high-protein, cholesterol-free tofu into your favorite recipes.

GETTING YOUR FAMILY STARTED

If you or members of your family are novices when it comes to eating or cooking with tofu, you may want to ease into the new adventure gradually.

Although, in a few weeks, you may rush home from the market with a cake of tofu, drain it, slice it, and enjoy it as is, many people enjoy their first tofu dishes without even realizing that they're eating tofu. One vegetarian food columnist regularly asks guests if they think her creamy shakes are made with ice cream or milk. Some think it's the former, others the latter—all ask for seconds—but none realize, until she tells them, that the shakes are made with neither ice cream nor milk. She has reported exclamations of surprise when she confides that they are made from tofu and the milk of nuts. No cream. No milk. No cholesterol. And little fat.

If you're just starting to experiment with tofu, you may want to keep it a secret at first. Make tofu Sloppy Joes, chili, or shakes. Let your family enjoy them. And then surprise them by telling them about your special ingredient. Few people realize just how much seasoning, spices, and texture have to do with the overall taste of food. Tofu inexpensively and healthfully mimics the texture of eggs, meat, fish, or fowl in many dishes so effectively that most people cannot distinguish between foods prepared with tofu and those prepared with traditional ingredients.

Like many other protein foods, tofu can be baked, broiled, barbequed, grilled, fried, boiled, or steamed. Here are a few quick tips that might inspire your creative genius when it comes to using tofu:

Tofu inexpensively and healthfully mimics the taste and texture of eggs, meat, fish, and fowl. And most people won't even notice the difference!

- Tofu makes an excellent extender for tuna, chicken salads, or casseroles.
- Plain or marinated tofu goes nicely in almost any salad—tossed, potato, Waldorf, etc.
- Tofu lowers the amount of cholesterol you receive when you have scrambled eggs. Use 50 percent firm or soft tofu and 50 percent eggs. Just mash the tofu with your fork and add it to the egg batter.
- Pan-fried tofu is excellent in sandwiches.
- Blended soft or silken tofu makes a delicious base for salad dressings or dips.
- Tofu cubes can be blended in a soup for a creamed variety.
- A wide assortment of desserts can begin with a half pound of silken or soft tofu. Just blend with fresh fruit, add natural flavorings, such as vanilla, and mix with orange juice concentrate.

BASICS: MARINATING AND PAN-FRYING TOFU

Marinating tofu is a simple way to give it flavor. The recipes presented later in this chapter include a variety of delicious marinades. All you have to do is slice or cube your tofu, and put it in the marinade for an hour, a few hours, or even overnight—depending on the recipe and on your taste buds.

When you marinate meat, it is often to tenderize it. But tofu is already tender, so it does not need to be marinated for an extended period of time. Remember that it's best to marinate tofu in the refrigerator, since it is perishable.

Marinades can be as creative as your imagination. What about a marmalade marinade? Or teriyaki? Or honey? Or garlic? The variations are endless.

Marinated tofu can be eaten as is, or, for a remarkably meaty taste, it can be fried in oil. Fried tofu makes a tasty sandwich filling. Slices that are very thick may even remind you of fried chicken. The slices can be dipped in seasoned flour first, or dipped first in beaten egg and then in seasoned bread crumbs. For added flavor, try sprinkling some soy sauce onto the pan while cooking.

For information on choosing oils for marinating, frying, and other cooking techniques, see page 63.

Marinated tofu has a delicious flavor. Try frying it—or, for a healthful treat, eat it as is!

SUBSTITUTION: TOFU AS A HIDDEN, HEALTHY INGREDIENT

Tofu can be simmered in tomato sauce, or blended into a broccoli and onion quiche. It can steam from inside a homemade vegetable pot pie. Properly seasoned with garlic, basil, and parsley, tofu can even replace ricotta cheese in lasagna.

In the next section, we'll give you a few pointers on how to substitute tofu in beef, poultry, seafood, or egg recipes. But these are just our ideas. Remember that tofu has been called one of the most versatile foods in the world. Be creative. Let these ideas spur originals of your own. There are hundreds of dishes you can prepare using tofu. Tofu, for instance, makes a great base for a dip. There are, of course, tofu dips and dressings, like those from Nasoya, that you can buy ready-made in the store. But, it's also fun to use your imagination and substitute tofu for sour cream or mayonnaise in your favorite homemade or packaged dry dips.

If tofu is mixed with an equal amount of wheat or other grain, and seasoned, it can be shaped into delicious burgers. Tofu blended with cider or orange juice makes great thick shakes. A seasoned tofu-and-breadcrumb mixture is a perfect stuffing for bell peppers. Slicing or cubing tofu and mixing it with vegetables and seasonings makes a lean and mean stir-fry.

Toss tofu into your favorite casserole in place of meat, without changing the sauce or seasoning, and most people will not be able to tell the difference. Chop it into your special stuffing recipes. These dishes, like most made with tofu, will have no added cholesterol, and will be lower in calories than the foods they replace.

EGGS

Yeast breads, quick breads, and cakes can all be made with tofu instead of cholesterol-high eggs.

Lately, many of us have been warned to limit our consumption of eggs because of their high cholesterol content. But many recipes call for eggs. They not only are used in breakfast dishes, but are hidden in many baked goods as well. Fortunately, tofu can be as versatile as eggs—as you'll see in many of the recipes that follow.

As a rule, yeast breads, quick breads, and cakes can be made with tofu instead of eggs. It is best to use soft or silken tofu. Generally, for most recipes, you should substitute ⅓–¼ cup mashed tofu for one egg.

With some of the substitution dishes we mention, we can't stress enough that there is often a psychological component that comes into focus. When a tofu shake looks exactly like a milk shake, it may be enjoyed more than if it looked unfamiliar. And, if tofu scramble looks like scrambled eggs, it is more apt to be accepted.

Sometimes, just adding a few colorful seasonings can make tofu dishes look and taste more like the dishes they emulate. When making tofu scramble, for example, adding a bit of curry and tumeric will convince most people that they are really eating scrambled eggs.

BEEF, POULTRY, AND SEAFOOD

When using tofu in place of beef, poultry, or seafood, simply substitute tofu pound for pound for the original ingredient.

Most of the accomplished tofu cooks we talked to have good news regarding substituting tofu for beef, poultry, or seafood in many recipes: Simply use common sense, and substitute tofu pound for pound for what the recipe calls for. When substituting tofu for meat, poultry, or seafood, it is generally best to use firm or extra firm tofu. It resembles their textures more closely.

When substituting tofu for ground beef, you may want to freeze the tofu first, as we described earlier, and then sauté it in seasonings, olive oil, and soy sauce. When crumbled, the texture of the tofu will closely resemble that of hamburger meat.

Some of the best tofu dishes are made with recipes that call for chunks of chicken or poultry. Fried, chunked firm, extra firm, or herbed tofu can step onto center stage without most diners batting an eye.

When converting a seafood recipe, consider the type of fish that you would have used, and slice and prepare the tofu similarly. Tofu works exceptionally well in seafood dishes that are prepared with sauces.

SO, YOU DON'T FEEL LIKE COOKING TONIGHT?

At this point, we hope you feel confident in your knowledge of tofu. You know how to boil it, broil it, freeze it, store it, drain it, grill it, blend it, slice it, and even whip up a batch from scratch.

If, perhaps, you don't feel like cooking, why not go to a local Japanese restaurant, or a restaurant specializing in vegetarian dishes? This would be a great way for you and your family to discover just how versatile tofu can be. You may get inspired and decide to imitate some of your favorite tofu restaurant dishes at home. Or, perhaps it's time to discover all of the diverse convenience products that are based on or include tofu. Many are already lining the shelves of your supermarkets and health food stores, and many more are scheduled to arrive in the near future.

So, if you decide to try some new tofu products, you'll have plenty to choose from. According to the Soyfoods Center of Lafayette, California, largely due to the popularity of tofu, soy food product introductions reached an all-time high in 1987, when 330 new soy products were introduced. In the last ten years, sales have increased over 600 percent!

You can now fill your shopping cart and satisfy your family's appetite with Tofu Pups—an uncommon dog from Lightlife Foods that many swear is a hot dog. Legume brand low- or no-cholesterol frozen meals are also available in many markets. Some of the choices include Manicotti Florentine, Vegetable Lasagna, Round Ravioli, Mexicana Enchiladas, and Stuffed Shells.

Soyco offers many cheese replacements. Soymage tofu cheeses with milk protein include Cheddar Style, Mozzarella Style, Monterey Jack Style, American Cheddar Style Singles, Cream Cheese Style, and Grated Parmesan Style.

Nasoya, as we've mentioned, has been a leader in the development of tofu-based shelf-stable products. Nayonaise, the all-natural cholesterol-free tofu mayonnaise replacement, has proved very popular. Italian, Creamy Dill, Garden Herb, and Sesame Garlic Vegi-dressings also have enthusiastic followers. Recently, Nasoya introduced a line of cholesterol-free tofu-stuffed pasta products, as well.

Some of the pioneer supermarket tofu products—which clearly label tofu as their main ingredient—are still going strong, too. To-futti, which many people prefer to ice cream, is widely available, as are a number of other ice cream-replacement products that are made with soy and tofu.

Your local health food store or supermarket may be the best place to find a wide variety of tofu-based products. Try tofu hot dogs, tofu-stuffed pasta shells, tofu ice cream, and even tofu chocolates!

Legume recently introduced their new gourmet tofu-based chocolates. Legume uses Sucanat, a granulated cane juice, instead of sugar, when preparing these treats. Among the chocolates available are Barat Tofu Chocolate Bars in Plain, Almond, Almond and California Raisin, and Truffle with Praline. Barat Tofu Chocolate Bits, Smothered Raisins, Dipped Peanuts, and Mints are also widely sold.

Smothered Raisins? Dipped Peanuts? Mints? It's doubtful that the Buddhist missionaries who first transported the soybean from China to Japan in 200 A.D. would have imagined that thousands of years later, Westerners would be watching something called *Rambo* or *Ghostbusters* and sticking their hand into a box of chocolate-covered tofu raisins for a mid-movie snack!

Amy's Kitchen, a northern California company, recently introduced a number of frozen meals featuring tofu. One of the most popular is Amy's Organic Vegetable Pot Pie. What's interesting about many of these products—which are the "New Wave" of tofu products—is that their existence and the way that they are labeled show how mainstream tofu has become. A few years ago, you would probably have had to search just to find *plain* tofu. Any product that contained tofu—packaged tofu burgers or frozen meals, for instance—was probably clearly labeled as such so that only true tofu aficionados would purchase it.

Today, products like Amy's Organic Vegetable Pot Pie barely even show that tofu is an ingredient, although some do display a colorful picture of a portion of tofu on the box. Nasoya's Nayonaise and Vegi-dressings don't mention tofu anywhere on their front labels. Instead, the words "100 percent cholesterol-free" are prominently displayed. A large segment of the public has become so health-conscious that "cholesterol-free" is stressed in most packaging. Most of the people interested in natural foods are already aware of the benefits of tofu, and have helped to bring it into the mainstream—where it is just an ingredient (albeit, a super healthy one) listed on the back of a package.

A WORD ABOUT OILS

When choosing oils to use in your tofu recipes—and in all the foods you make—you should consider two things: the desired flavor of the dish, and the method of cooking being used.

Each oil has a distinctive flavor, and sometimes a particular oil is used to lend its special taste to a particular dish. When preparing Italian food, for instance, you may enjoy the traditional flavor of olive oil, while Oriental dishes will taste most authentic if sesame oil is used. By trying different oils, you'll discover which best complements your favorite foods.

Most of us know that certain polyunsaturated oils are the healthiest choices for salads and other dishes that require no cooking. Corn, olive, safflower, sesame, soy, and sunflower oils are all excellent choices for dishes of this type. In fact, recent studies have indicated that olive oil can actually help *lower* the level of cholesterol in the body. When buying this and other oils, try to find unrefined, naturally extracted (cold-pressed) oils, as these are the most flavorful, the most digestible, and the most nutritious.

What you may *not* know is that not all of the oils suitable for uncooked foods are best when cooking. When using heat, you'll want to choose oils that remain stable at higher temperatures. These oils not only produce more flavorful results, without burning or smoking during preparation, but are also more healthful. When sautéeing, or doing any cooking at relatively low temperatures, it is best to choose olive, safflower, sunflower, or sesame oil. When cooking at higher temperatures—when deep-frying, for instance— safflower and sunflower oils will yield the best results.

When you decided to add tofu to your diet, you made a great start in providing your family with healthier, delicious meals. By purchasing good-quality oils, and carefully selecting the oil used to prepare each of your tofu dishes, you'll insure optimal nutrition and taste in all the foods you serve.

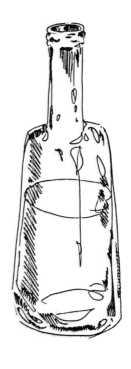

SWEETENER EQUIVALENTS

Before you start experimenting with all the tempting tofu recipes we have collected for you, you might want to take a look at the following list. A number of our tofu recipes call for a sweetener. Our list will allow you to easily substitute one natural sweetener for another.

The sweeteners in the list are all gluten free, except for maltose and barley malt extract, which should not be used if following a gluten-free diet.

Remember that you must always decrease or increase the amount of liquid or dry ingredients in a recipe according to the liquid content of the sweetener. For instance, if you use 1¼ cups maltose to take the place of ½ cup of another sweetener, you should either decrease the liquid in the recipe by ¾ cup, or add flour, ground nuts, seeds, coconut, or arrowroot to balance the added liquid.

If you choose to use the dried fruit purée, you can use any of the following fruits: nectarines, peaches, apricots, mangoes, raisins, currants, figs, dates, Chinese dates, pineapples, and bananas.

By experimenting, you'll find out which of the sweeteners you and your family prefer, and which of the sweeteners best complements the ingredients in each of your favorite recipes.

½ cup sweetener is equal to:

- ½ cup maple syrup
- ½ cup honey
- ⅓ cup molasses
- ½ cup coconut sugar
- 1¼ cups maltose
- 1½ cups barley malt extract
- ½ cup fruit juice concentrate
- 1 cup sugarless fruit jam or jelly
- 1¼ cups rice syrup
- 1¼ cups dried fruit purée
- 2 cups fruit juice
- 1 cup fruit juice and 1 cup carrot juice
- ½ cup unsweetened frozen juice concentrate

SALADS

BEET POTATO SALAD

SERVES 4

3 large beets, peeled and cubed
1 large potato, peeled and cubed
½ pound firm tofu, cubed
½ cup celery, diced
½ cup Tofu Mayonnaise (see page 75 for recipe)
1 teaspoon prepared horseradish

1. Steam or boil beets and potato until tender.
2. Drain vegetables, and combine with tofu and celery.
3. Dress with Tofu Mayonnaise and horseradish.
4. Chill before serving.

POTATO SALAD

SERVES 6

3 cups potatoes, cooked and diced
1 pound extra firm tofu, diced
1 cup chopped vegetables (green peppers, celery, or
summer squash are good)
¼ cup minced onion or 2 tablespoons chopped chives
¼ cup pickles or green olives, chopped
2 tablespoons fresh parsley, minced
¾ cup Tofu Mayonnaise (see page 75 for recipe)
1 teaspoon curry powder
2 teaspoons prepared mustard
¼ teaspoon pepper
½ teaspoon salt
1 clove garlic (crushed) or ¼ teaspoon garlic powder

1. In a large bowl, mix together potatoes, tofu, vegetables of your choice, onion or chives, pickles or olives, and parsley.

2. In a separate bowl, blend the Tofu Mayonnaise, curry powder, mustard, salt, pepper, and garlic.
3. Combine dressing with vegetables.
4. Chill and serve.

ONION AND RADISH SALAD

2 cups sliced onion rings
2 bunches red radishes, cut into thin circles
1 cup celery, chopped
Radishes and sprouts (as garnish)

PARSLEY DRESSING
1 cup parsley, chopped
½ pound soft tofu
1 tablespoon lemon juice
½ teaspoon crushed garlic
1 tablespoon tahini
2 tablespoons vinegar
¼ cup olive oil
Sea salt to taste

1. Bring a large pot of water to a boil.
2. Add salt.
3. Blanch onion rings for 3 minutes. Drain.
4. Arrange the onions, radishes, and celery in layers in a glass serving bowl.
5. Chop parsley and process with other dressing ingredients in blender, adjusting liquid content if necessary.
6. Pour dressing over vegetables, and garnish with sliced radishes and sprouts.

TOFU WALDORF SALAD

SERVES 4

4 tablespoons agar or 1 envelope unflavored gelatin
¼ cup sweetener
1½ cups apple juice
3 teaspoons lemon juice
1 teaspoon Worcestershire sauce (optional)
½ teaspoon celery seed
1½ cups red apples, peeled and diced
1 cup celery, diced
½ cup chopped walnuts or toasted sunflower seeds

DRESSING
1 tablespoon agar or ¼ envelope unflavored gelatin
¼ cup apple juice
½ pound soft tofu
½ cup Tofu Mayonnaise (see page 75 for recipe)
1 tablespoon sweetener

1. In a saucepan, mix 4 tablespoons agar (soak first for a few minutes), ¼ cup sweetener, 1½ cups apple juice, lemon juice, Worcestershire sauce, and celery seed. Heat for 5 minutes, stirring constantly. Then chill mixture for 15 minutes.
2. Fold apples, celery, and walnuts or sunflower seeds into mixture, and pour into a mold. Set aside.
3. In a saucepan, mix 1 tablespoon agar and ¼ cup apple juice. Heat for 5 minutes, stirring constantly.
4. Blend the agar and apple juice mixture with the tofu, Tofu Mayonnaise, and sweetener.
5. Pour dressing over mixture in mold. Chill, and serve.

SERVES 4–6

BUCKWHEAT NOODLE SALAD

6 large Japanese or Chinese dried mushrooms
½ pound firm tofu
2 tablespoons brown rice vinegar
2 tablespoons lemon or orange juice
½–1 teaspoon sea salt
4–6 tablespoons olive oil
Minced onions (optional)
Minced parsley or basil (optional)
2 teaspoons prepared mustard (optional)
2 cups quartered zucchini, cut into 1-inch lengths
2 cups carrots, sliced
1 cup shelled peas
½ cup water or stock (use soaking water from mushrooms)
1 tablespoon soy sauce
2 tablespoons mirin
½ pound buckwheat noodles
1 cup scallions, minced (as garnish)

1. Place mushrooms in bowl. Boil water and pour over mushrooms to cover. Soak until tender.
2. Drain mushrooms, reserving liquid. Discard stems, and slice mushrooms fine. Set aside.
3. Combine tofu with next four ingredients, processing in blender until creamy. Add onions, parsley, and mustard, if desired.
4. Steam or blanch zucchini, carrots, and peas for 2–3 minutes in salted water. Drain and rinse.
5. Combine reserved water, soy sauce, and mirin. Add sliced mushrooms, and boil uncovered until almost dry.
6. Cook noodles in boiling water until al dente, 8–9 minutes. Drain and rinse under cold running water.
7. Toss salad with mushroom mixture. Then arrange salad on individual plates, and pour dressing on top. Garnish with scallions.

HERBED TOFU GARDEN SALAD

SERVES 4

½ cup olive oil
¼ cup wine vinegar
1 teaspoon salt
½ teaspoon dried basil
1 teaspoon tarragon
Pinch pepper
1 pound asparagus, cooked and cut up
¼ pound mushrooms, sliced thin
1 small red onion, sliced thin
2 small zucchini, sliced thin
¼ pound cherry tomatoes
1 pound extra firm tofu, sliced into thin strips

1. In a large salad bowl, combine olive oil, wine vinegar, salt, basil, tarragon, and pepper.
2. Add asparagus, mushrooms, onion, zucchini, tomatoes, and tofu. Stir mixture gently to coat vegetables.
3. Cover and chill several hours before serving. This is especially good when served with French bread.

HERBED TOFU CUBES

SERVES 4

1 cup olive oil
¼ cup lemon juice
2 tablespoons scallions, minced
1 clove garlic, minced
1 teaspoon basil, crumbled
1 pound firm tofu, cut into 1-inch cubes

1. In a 1-quart jar, combine oil, lemon juice, scallions, garlic, and basil.
2. Cover jar, and shake well.
3. Pour mixture over tofu cubes, and marinate overnight in refrigerator.
4. Serve cubes over salad, cook with vegetables, or eat as is.

CARROT SALAD WITH CREAMY TOFU DRESSING

SERVES 4

1 pound carrots, grated or thinly sliced
¼ cup raisins
¼ cup chopped walnuts or toasted sunflower seeds
½ pound firm tofu
2 tablespoons lemon juice or vinegar
2 tablespoons sweetener
1 teaspoon salt
¼ teaspoon ginger powder
¼ teaspoon celery seed

1. In a bowl, combine carrots, raisins, and walnuts or sunflower seeds.
2. In a blender, process tofu, lemon juice or vinegar, sweetener, salt, ginger, and celery seed until smooth.
3. Combine the two mixtures, and serve.

THAI SALAD

SERVES 4

3 tablespoons nam pla (Siamese seasoning), optional
2 tablespoons natural sweetener
Juice of 2 limes
1 pound firm tofu, cubed
2 cups peanuts, roasted and coarsely chopped
½ head of lettuce, shredded
½ pound bean sprouts
3 tablespoons fresh basil, coarsely chopped
3 tablespoons fresh mint, coarsely chopped
3 tablespoons fresh coriander, coarsley chopped

1. Mix nam pla, sweetener, and lime juice.
2. Marinate tofu cubes in above mixture for 15 minutes.
3. Toss tofu-marinade mixture with remaining ingredients, and serve.

TOFU TUNA PLATE

SERVES 4

1 6-ounce can tuna
1 tablespoon pimento
1 tablespoon parsley, minced
1 tablespoon celery, chopped
3 drops Tabasco sauce
½ teaspoon dry mustard
½ pound soft tofu
Toast or crackers
Dill pickle slices (as garnish)

1. Mix tuna, pimento, parsley, celery, Tabasco sauce, mustard, and tofu.
2. Chill mixture for 2 hours.
3. Serve with toast or crackers, garnished with dill pickle slices.

CHILLED PEPPER AND TOFU SALAD

SERVES 4

3 red or green peppers
½ teaspoon dried basil
1 clove garlic, minced
1 tablespoon olive oil
5 scallions, cut into 1-inch lengths
½ pound firm tofu, cut into ½-inch cubes
2 teaspoons soy sauce
¼ cup water
1 tablespoon vinegar

1. Slice peppers in rings and remove seeds. Slice each ring in half.
2. Stir-fry peppers, basil, and garlic in a medium-sized saucepan for 5 minutes, using olive oil.
3. Add scallions, tofu, soy sauce, and water.
4. Bring to boil, lower heat, and simmer for about 10 minutes, or until water is evaporated.
5. Add vinegar, and remove pan from heat.
6. Refrigerate for at least 1 hour before serving to allow salad to marinate. Serve chilled.

TOFU TUNA SALAD

SERVES 4

1 6-ounce can tuna, drained
3 tablespoons Tofu Mayonnaise (see page 75 for recipe)
4 ounces firm tofu, diced
¼ cup dill pickles, minced
1 tablespoon fresh parsley, minced

1. Combine all ingredients in a bowl and serve.

DRESSINGS & DIPS

GUACAMOLE

SERVES 4–6

1 ripe avocado, peeled and pitted
4 ounces soft tofu
1 clove garlic or ¼ teaspoon garlic powder
1 tablespoon lemon juice
⅛ teaspoon salt
¼ teaspoon ground coriander (optional)
¼ teaspoon chili powder (optional)
½ teaspoon Worcestershire sauce (optional)
1 small tomato, chopped

1. In a blender or food processor, blend together avocado, tofu, garlic, lemon juice, salt, coriander, chili powder, and Worcestershire sauce until smooth.
2. Place mixture in bowl, stir in chopped tomato, and serve.

BLUE CHEESE DRESSING

SERVES 4–6

4 ounces firm tofu
1 teaspoon minced onion
1 teaspoon dry mustard
½ teaspoon salt
Dash pepper
1½ tablespoons vinegar
¼ cup vegetable oil
2 to 4 ounces blue cheese

1. In a blender, mix tofu, minced onion, dry mustard, salt, pepper, and vinegar until smooth.
2. While blending, slowly add vegetable oil.
3. Stop blender and stir in 2 to 4 ounces blue cheese. Serve.

SERVES 4–6

"SAFFRON" TOFU DRESSING

½ pound soft tofu, mashed
2 teaspoons tumeric
2 tablespoons lemon or lime juice
1 small cucumber, peeled and diced
Soy milk (optional)

1. Pound, purée, or process all ingredients until smooth.
2. Thin with soy milk, if necessary, and serve.

SERVES 4–6

LIME TOFU SAUCE

½ pound soft tofu, mashed
½ bunch parsley, chopped fine
4 tablespoons lime juice
2 tablespoons tahini or 1 tablespoon sesame purée
1 tablespoon white miso

1. Place parsley in a cheesecloth, and squeeze juice into tofu.
2. Dip cloth in lime juice, and again wring and squeeze out into tofu until tofu is pale green. Discard parsley.
3. Purée tofu with remaining ingredients. Serve with seafood.

SERVES 12

TOMATOFU DIP

1 tablespoon cider vinegar (pickle vinegar from onions works well, too)
1 teaspoon ginger, finely grated
½ pound soft tofu, mashed
2 medium ripe tomatoes, skinned and seeded,
or 2 tablespoons tomato paste
Salt to taste
Freshly ground black pepper

1. Mix cider vinegar and ginger, and allow to sit for 5 minutes.
2. Pound, purée, or process all ingredients until smooth. Serve with Deep-Fried Tofu Rolls. (See page 104 for recipe.)

POPPY SEED TOFU DIP

SERVES 12

½ pound soft tofu, mashed
2 tablespoons tahini
2 tablespoons light miso
2 tablespoons vinegar or lemon juice
¼–½ cup water
2 tablespoons poppy seeds
2 tablespoons chopped parsley

1. In a blender, blend tofu, tahini, miso, vinegar or lemon juice, and water.
2. In a skillet, gently roast poppy seeds, stirring constantly to prevent burning.
3. When seeds have a nutty aroma, add to the tofu mixture.
4. Add parsley, and serve.

TOFU MAYONNAISE

SERVES 12

½ pound soft tofu
1 cup water
2 tablespoons olive or corn oil
2 tablespoons vinegar
2 tablespoons fresh lemon juice
¼ teaspoon sea salt
¼ teaspoon ground coriander

1. Combine ingredients in a blender and purée until creamy, stopping blender periodically to push contents down with a rubber spatula. Refrigerated, this mayonnaise will keep for 2 days. If the mixture separates, stir well to combine.

MISO TAHINI SANDWICH SPREAD

SERVES 4–6

4 ounces soft tofu
4 tablespoons tahini
2 tablespoons miso
Green olives, chopped (optional)

1. Mash tofu, tahini, and miso in bowl.
2. Stir in olives, if desired, and serve.

TOFU HUMMUS

SERVES 12

½ pound soft or silken tofu
½ cup tahini
½ cup lemon juice
1 cup chickpeas, cooked
1 teaspoon salt
2 medium cloves garlic
Pocket bread (pita), optional

1. In a blender or food processor, blend tofu, tahini, lemon juice, chickpeas, salt, and garlic until smooth. Hummus is traditionally served with pieces of pocket bread.

DILL TOFU DIP

SERVES 4–6

½ pound soft tofu, mashed
3–4 gherkins, chopped
1 tablespoon chopped fresh dill
2 teaspoons honey
1 tablespoon lemon juice

1. Mash, purée, or blend all ingredients until smooth.
2. Chill. Serve with corn chips or rice crackers.

CREAMY ITALIAN DRESSING SERVES 12

½ pound firm tofu
½ cup water
4 tablespoons olive oil
3 tablespoons lemon juice or vinegar
2 cloves garlic or ½ teaspoon garlic powder
½ teaspoon onion powder
1 teaspoon Italian herbs
1 tablespoon parsley
¼ teaspoon salt

1. In a blender, blend all ingredients until smooth, and serve.

LEMON AND GARLIC SAUCE SERVES 12

1 pound firm tofu
3–4 tablespoons lemon juice to taste
1 tablespoon prepared mustard
½ teaspoon pressed garlic
2 tablespoons tahini
Sea salt to taste

1. Drop tofu into boiling water. Remove quickly.
2. Combine tofu with other ingredients in a blender, and process until smooth.

TOFU SOUR CREAM SERVES 4–6

½ pound soft tofu
¼ cup oil
4 tablespoons lemon juice
1 teaspoon sea salt
½ cup chopped parsley (optional)

1. In a blender, combine tofu with the rest of the dressing ingredients, except for parsley.
2. Stir in parsley to give sour cream a green color.
3. Taste and adjust seasoning, and serve.

SERVES 12

GREEN GODDESS DRESSING

½ pound firm tofu
½ cup Tofu Mayonnaise (see page 75 for recipe)
⅓ cup parsley, chopped
1 clove garlic
3 tablespoons lemon juice
¼ teaspoon paprika
¼ teaspoon salt
½ teaspoon prepared mustard
2 tablespoons vegetable oil (optional)

1. In a blender, blend all ingredients until smooth, and serve.

SERVES 12

HORSERADISH DIP

3 tablespoons freshly grated horseradish
½ pound firm tofu, mashed
1 tablespoon vegetable oil
¼ teaspoon salt
1 teaspoon lemon juice
2 tablespoons parsley or watercress, minced

1. In a blender, mix horseradish, tofu, oil, salt, and lemon juice until smooth.
2. Add parsley or watercress, and serve.

SOUPS

Tofu Miso Soup

SERVES 2

1 tablespoon vegetable oil
1½ cups leeks or onions, chopped
1 carrot, thinly sliced
2 cups water
2-inch piece wakame seaweed
2 tablespoons miso, dissolved in 3 tablespoons water
8 ounces silken tofu, cubed
Parsley or scallions (as garnish)

1. Sauté carrots and leeks or onions in vegetable oil over medium heat until tender.
2. Add water and wakame seaweed, and bring to a boil.
3. Reduce heat.
4. Stir in miso and tofu.
5. Garnish with parsley or scallions, and serve.

Borscht

SERVES 4–6

4 beets, peeled and sliced
3–4 cups chicken stock
2 tablespoons vinegar
2 tablespoons finely chopped parsley
2 tablespoons finely chopped dill
Several tablespoons Tofu Sour Cream (see page 77 for recipe)

1. In pot, combine beets with hot stock. Bring stock to a boil, cover, and simmer 10 minutes.
2. Remove soup from pot, and purée along with the vinegar.
3. Put purée back in pot, add herbs, and warm. Taste and adjust seasoning.
4. Serve hot or cold, with a spoonful of Tofu Sour Cream in the center of the soup.

CREAM OF MUSHROOM-CHICKEN SOUP

SERVES 8

4 tablespoons olive oil
5 cloves garlic, coarsely chopped
2 bay leaves
2 pounds mushrooms, chopped
1 teaspoon sea salt
1 teaspoon basil
5 cups chicken stock
3 tablespoons miso or 1 teaspoon salt
Freshly ground black pepper
½ pound silken tofu
Squeeze of lemon juice

1. Heat the oil in a large saucepan over high heat.
2. When it is very hot, add garlic and bay leaves.
3. Stir briefly and add mushrooms. Cook over high heat for 5 minutes.
4. Add 1 teaspoon of sea salt, cover, and simmer rapidly for 15 minutes, stirring occasionally. The mushrooms should lose most of their liquid.
5. Add the basil and chicken stock, and return mixture to a boil. Simmer for 5 minutes.
6. Strain the soup, and pound, purée, or process the solids with a little of the liquid and the miso. Mix into the soup, and simmer for 5 minutes before serving.
7. Add black pepper to taste.
8. Purée tofu with a little lemon juice and water.
9. Swirl 1 tablespoon of puréed tofu mixture into each bowl of soup, and serve.

VARIATION

- For a change of pace, use vegetable-seaweed stock instead of chicken stock.

SILKEN MUSHROOM SOUP WITH WINE

SERVES 4

3 tablespoons vegetable oil
½ pound mushrooms, finely chopped
1 small onion, diced
1 stalk celery, sliced
1 clove garlic, chopped
2 cups water
1 pound silken tofu
1 teaspoon salt
¼ teaspoon paprika
⅛ teaspoon nutmeg
3 to 4 tablespoons dry white wine

1. Heat oil in a large skillet. Add mushrooms, onions, celery, and garlic, and sauté 5 minutes.
2. In a bowl, mix sautéed vegetables with water, tofu, salt, paprika, nutmeg, and wine. Place mixture in blender, and process until smooth.
3. Pour mixture into a large pot, simmer 15 minutes, and serve.

CLEAR SOUP WITH TOFU AND WATERCRESS

SERVES 4

1 strip kombu seaweed, 6–8 inches long,
soaked in water 5 minutes
4–5 cups water
Tamari
1 cup soft tofu, cubed
½ bunch fresh watercress, washed

1. Place kombu and water in pot and bring to a boil, uncovered.
2. Reduce heat to medium-low, cover pot, and simmer several minutes.

3. Remove kombu and set it aside for use in other dishes or soups.
4. Season the water with a little tamari, and simmer 5 minutes.
5. Add tofu cubes and simmer additional 2 minutes.
6. Place 1 or 2 sprigs of fresh watercress in individual bowls.
7. Pour the hot soup over the watercress, and serve.

BEAN CURD AND COCONUT SOUP

SERVES 4

2 whole stalks lemongrass or 1 teaspoon lemongrass powder
2 teaspoons Laos powder (or ginger root)
Milk from 1 coconut or 1 tin increased to 1½ quarts with water
1 pound firm tofu, diced
½ cup white miso
1 chili, seeded and sliced in thin rounds
Juice of 1 lime
2 tablespoons fresh basil or mint, finely chopped,
or 1 tablespoon of each
1 tablespoon nam pla (Siamese seasoning), optional
Fresh coriander (as garnish)

1. Chop lemongrass, and bruise it with the flat of a cleaver.
2. Add Laos powder and lemongrass to coconut milk, and slowly bring to a boil while stirring gently. Simmer for 10 minutes.
3. Strain off lemongrass.
4. Add tofu, stirring into stock.
5. Remove 2 cups of stock. Dissolve miso in it, and return to pot. Simmer for 5 minutes.
6. Add remaining ingredients, and serve garnished with coriander. This is delicious with a bowl of Thai jasmine rice.

TOMATO SOUP

SERVES 4

2 cups fresh or canned tomatoes, chopped
½ cup celery, chopped
¼ cup onions, chopped
1 bay leaf (remove before blending)
1 teaspoon basil
½ teaspoon salt
¼ teaspoon pepper
1 pound silken tofu
3 tablespoons vegetable oil (preferably olive)
Croutons (as garnish)

1. In pot, mix together tomatoes, celery, onions, bay leaf, basil, salt, and pepper. Cover, and simmer for about 15 minutes.
2. Blend in tofu and oil.
3. Serve hot or cold, garnished with croutons if desired.

GAZPACHO

SERVES 2

2 large fresh tomatoes
1 clove garlic
¼ cup olive oil
2 tablespoons lemon juice
⅓ cup fresh parsley and/or celery leaves, chives,
chervil, and basil (optional)
1 teaspoon salt
½ pound silken tofu
1 cup water
2 cups diced fresh vegetable of your choice
(onion, cucumber, corn, peas, summer squash, peppers, etc.)

1. In a blender, blend tomatoes, garlic, oil, lemon juice, parsley, salt and other seasonings, tofu, and water.
2. Pour the mixture into a large bowl, and add the vegetables of your choice.
3. Chill the soup for at least 2 hours before serving.

SERVES 4

VIETNAMESE MINT SOUP

2 cups chicken stock
½ pound firm tofu, chopped
¼ pound cooked chicken, diced
2 tablespoons soy sauce
Pinch cayenne
1 tablespoon chopped Vietnamese mint

1. Bring stock to a boil.
2. Stir in tofu and chicken, and simmer until hot.
3. Season with soy sauce, cayenne, and mint, and serve at once.

VARIATION

- If you can't find Vietnamese mint, coriander can be used as a substitute. Either of these herbs will impart a delicate aroma to this delicious soup.

SERVES 4

CREAMY TOFU SOUP

½ pound silken tofu
4 cups water
3 celery stalks, diced
1 medium onion, diced
½ teaspoon dark sesame oil
1 teaspoon sea salt
1 teaspoon dried dill
1 tablespoon whole-wheat pastry or unbleached white flour
1 tablespoon kuzu
1–2 scallions, chopped (as garnish)

1. Purée tofu in a blender with 1 cup of water (reserving the remaining 3 cups), and pour mixture into a 2-quart or larger saucepan.
2. Sauté celery and onion in oil until onion is pearly white, adding sea salt while sautéing.

3. Add sautéed vegetables, 3 cups water, and dill to puréed tofu.
4. Combine flour, kuzu, and small amount of soup in a small bowl, and stir until smooth.
5. Stir kuzu mixture into soup and heat over low flame for 30 minutes, stirring often. Soup will thicken.
6. Serve hot, garnished with chopped scallions.

MISO WITH GREENS

SERVES 4–6

6 cups water
1 stick kombu seaweed
1 large or 2 medium to small bok choy (Chinese cabbage),
washed well and sliced
3–4 tablespoons brown rice or barley miso
1 teaspoon finely grated ginger
1 cup firm tofu, mashed

1. Bring water and kombu to a boil.
2. Remove kombu and discard, and add cabbage.
3. Over high heat, bring soup to a boil again. Simmer with lid on for 5 minutes.
4. Take out 1 cup stock, and mix with miso and ginger until miso is dissolved. Return stock to pot.
5. Add tofu, and stir well.
6. Simmer for 5 minutes, and serve.

VARIATION

• If Chinese greens are not available, use spinach, and add 2 tablespoons lemon juice along with the tofu.

ENTRÉES

SERVES 3–4

Tofu Lasagna

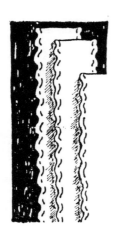

½ pound lasagna noodles
10 ounces spinach (optional)
2 tablespoons vegetable oil
1 medium onion, chopped
½ pound mushrooms
1 clove garlic, minced
1 pound firm tofu, mashed
½ cup grated Parmesan cheese or Romano cheese
2 beaten eggs (optional)
2 tablespoons parsley, chopped
½ teaspoon salt or 1 tablespoon soy sauce
¼ teaspoon pepper
3 cups spaghetti sauce
¼ cup grated mozzarella, Swiss, or Monterey Jack cheese

1. Cook lasagna noodles, drain, and set aside.
2. If you are using spinach, wash, chop, and steam lightly. Then set aside.
3. Sauté onion, mushrooms, and garlic in 2 tablespoons vegetable oil. Set aside.
4. In a bowl, mix together tofu, Parmesan or Romano cheese, eggs, parsley, salt or soy sauce, and pepper.
5. Mix together the sautéed vegetables and tofu mixture.
6. Oil an 8 x 11-inch baking dish.
7. Place a row of noodles on the bottom. Build layers, alternating noodles, tofu mixture, spaghetti sauce, spinach, and grated cheese. The final layer should be sauce.
8. Cover the dish with aluminum foil; bake in preheated oven at 350°F for 40 minutes.
9. Remove foil, bake another 10 minutes, and serve.

TOFU ITALIANO

SERVES 4–6

1 pound firm tofu
3 eggs, beaten
2 cups crushed tomatoes
¼ teaspoon garlic powder
1 teaspoon basil
¼ cup onions, chopped
¼ cup green peppers, chopped
Pinch nutmeg
¼ cup wheat flour
¼ teaspoon salt
Oil
½ cup Parmesan cheese

1. Combine tofu, eggs, tomatoes, garlic powder, basil, onions, green peppers, nutmeg, flour, and salt in a food processor or blender, and process until smooth.
2. Pour half of the mixture into an oiled baking pan, and sprinkle with ¼ cup of Parmesan cheese.
3. Add remaining mixture, and bake in preheated oven at 350°F for 50 minutes.
4. Sprinkle the rest of the Parmesan cheese on top, and return to oven long enough to brown the cheese. Serve.

TOFU PARMIGIANA

SERVES 4–6

2 pounds firm tofu, cut in ½-inch slices
2 tablespoons vegetable oil
3–4 cups spaghetti sauce
¾ to 1 pound mozzarella cheese, grated or sliced
Parmesan cheese, grated (optional)

1. Sauté tofu in vegetable oil until lightly browned.
2. Layer tofu in a baking dish with sauce and mozzarella cheese. Top final layer with a sprinkling of Parmesan cheese, if desired.
3. Bake in preheated oven at 350°F for 30 minutes. Serve.

TOFU SPAGHETTI SAUCE

SERVES 4

2 onions, diced
2 cloves garlic, minced, or ¼ teaspoon garlic powder
Vegetable oil
3 large tomatoes, diced
2 green peppers, diced
¼ pound mushrooms, sliced thin
1 carrot, grated or diced
1 cup water
1 bay leaf
1 pound extra firm tofu, cubed
3 tablespoons vegetable oil
½ teaspoon salt or 1 tablespoon soy sauce
Dash pepper

1. In a large pot or skillet, sauté onions and garlic in oil for 5 minutes.
2. Add tomatoes, green peppers, mushrooms, and carrot, and sauté another 3–4 minutes.
3. Add water, bay leaf, tofu, vegetable oil, salt, soy sauce, and pepper. Cover, and bring to a boil.
4. Reduce heat and simmer for 1 hour, stirring occasionally.

FETTUCCINE LERMANO

SERVES 2–3

¼ pound firm tofu
Water
2 cloves garlic, minced
2 tablespoons olive oil
1 umeboshi plum (pit removed) or 1 teaspoon umeboshi plum paste
½ teaspoon sea salt
¾–1 cup water
¼ teaspoon dry mustard
8 ounces artichoke, whole-wheat, or spinach fettuccine
¼ cup chopped parsley
3 tablespoons chopped green olives

1. Boil tofu in water to cover for 2 minutes, and drain.
2. Purée tofu, garlic, oil, umeboshi plum, sea salt, water, and mustard in a suribachi, blender, or food processor until smooth.
3. Heat tofu mixture in a medium-sized saucepan over a very low flame.
4. While sauce is heating, boil fettuccine for 8–10 minutes or until tender, and drain.
5. Toss fettuccine, tofu sauce, parsley, and olives together in large pot or mixing bowl. Transfer to platter, and serve hot.

NOODLES WITH DILL CAULIFLOWER SAUCE

SERVES 4

1 medium onion, chopped
1 teaspoon dried dill or 2 teaspoons fresh dill, chopped
1 tablespoon rice vinegar
½ teaspoon sea salt
¼ cup water
2 teaspoons kuzu
1 cup water
1 small head of cauliflower, broken into small flowerets (about 3 cups)
1 pound soft tofu, cubed
1 pound flat noodles
1 tablespoon toasted poppy seeds
Chopped parsley or scallions (as garnish)

1. Simmer onion, dill, rice vinegar, and sea salt in ¼ cup water until onions are transparent.
2. Dissolve kuzu in 1 cup water, and add to pot of vegetables. Stir over medium heat until thickened—about 5 minutes.
3. Steam cauliflower for about 10 minutes, or until lightly cooked.
4. Add cauliflower and tofu to vegetable sauce, and keep hot over very low flame.
5. Boil noodles in salted water for about 10 minutes or until tender. Drain and rinse.
6. Toss cooked, warm noodles with poppy seeds.
7. Serve cauliflower sauce over noodles, and garnish with chopped parsley or scallions, if desired.

SERVES 4

TOFU NOODLE CASSEROLE

¾ pound spiral noodles, cooked and drained
2 broccoli stalks, steamed and cut into small chunks
1 pound firm tofu, drained
1½ tablespoons light miso
1 tablespoon vinegar
1 tablespoon soy sauce
2 tablespoons tahini or sesame butter
2 tablespoons lemon juice
2 tablespoons kuzu, dissolved in 1½ cups water
2 cloves garlic
Chopped parsley (as garnish)

1. Oil a large, shallow baking dish. Line it with noodles and broccoli. Set aside.
2. Combine tofu, miso, vinegar, soy sauce, tahini, lemon juice, dissolved kuzu-water mixture, and garlic in blender or food processor, and blend until smooth.
3. Pour tofu mixture over noodles and broccoli, covering them completely.
4. Bake at 400°F for 40 minutes, or until top browns and cracks slightly.
5. Serve garnished with chopped parsley.

SERVES 4

TOFU, PASTA, AND OLIVES

1 pound soft tofu
2 medium onions, diced
2 cups chopped kale
2 tablespoons olive oil
3 tablespoons light miso
½ teaspoon ground bay leaf
2 cups black olives, sliced
1 pound udon, artichoke, whole-wheat, or soba noodles

1. Drop tofu into medium-sized saucepan of boiling water (enough to cover), and cook for 2–3 minutes. Remove from water, and set aside.

2. Sauté onions and kale in oil.
3. Put tofu, onion, and kale in a suribachi, and grind to a pasty consistency.
4. Add miso and bay leaf, and grind until blended. Stir in olives, and set aside.
5. Boil noodles for about 10 minutes, or until tender, and drain.
6. Combine tofu mixture with hot pasta and serve. If desired, pasta and tofu mixture may be placed in a 9-inch square or round baking dish and put under broiler for 3–5 minutes before serving. This will form a light, crusty topping.

SPINACH NOODLE BAKE

SERVES 4

1 pound fettuccine or fine noodles
4 tablespoons vegetable oil
1 medium onion, minced
1 pound fresh spinach, chopped, or
2 packages frozen spinach, thawed and chopped
½ pound mushrooms, sliced
1 teaspoon caraway seeds
1 pound soft tofu
¼ cup white wine (optional)
¼ cup soy milk or water
1 teaspoon salt
¼ teaspoon pepper
¼ teaspoon nutmeg
¼ cup grated Parmesan cheese

1. Boil noodles until tender but firm, drain, and set aside.
2. Sauté onion, spinach, mushrooms, and caraway seeds in oil. Set aside.
3. In a blender, mix tofu, wine, soy milk, salt, pepper, and nutmeg until smooth.
4. Combine noodles, spinach mixture, tofu mixture, and Parmesan cheese. Pour into oiled casserole dish, and bake in preheated oven at 400°F for 20 minutes. Serve.

SERVES 6 # *NOODLES IN BROTH WITH TOFU*

1 pound udon or Chinese noodles
6 cups cold water
2 sticks kombu seaweed
5 shiitake mushrooms, rinsed
1 carrot, sliced
2 cups Chinese greens, sliced
1 tablespoon mirin
Dark sesame oil
1 pound firm tofu, sliced
1 cup bean sprouts
Scallion slices (as garnish)
Soy sauce to taste
6 eggs (optional)
Black pepper
Nori seaweed (toasted), cut into strips

1. Cook noodles until tender. Rinse under cold water and drain. Set aside.
2. Add kombu, mushrooms, and carrot to 6 cups cold water. Bring to a boil slowly.
3. Remove kombu, and discard. Add Chinese greens and mirin to mushroom mixture.
4. Place some noodles in each bowl. Add ¼ teaspoon dark sesame oil to each serving, then add tofu, bean sprouts, scallions, and soy sauce.
5. Remove mushrooms from broth, slice, and divide between the bowls. Add hot broth.
6. Poach eggs in shallow water, and place one in each bowl. Grind lots of black pepper on top, and add nori strips.

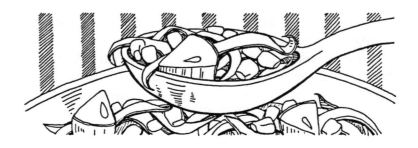

CHILI

2 pounds firm tofu, frozen
1 large onion, diced
2 cloves garlic, minced
2 tablespoons vegetable oil
4 cups cooked kidney beans (frozen, soaked, or canned)
3 cups tomatoes (canned or fresh), chopped
1–3 tablespoons chili powder, according to taste
1 teaspoon cumin
1 tablespoon vinegar
1 teaspoon sweetener
½–1½ teaspoons salt (use the lesser amount if the beans were salted)
¼ teaspoon black pepper
Cayenne pepper or Tabasco sauce, if desired

1. Thaw tofu. When thawed, press and crumble.
2. Sauté onion and garlic in vegetable oil. When onions are tender, add tofu, and sauté another few minutes.
3. In a large pot, mix all the ingredients and simmer for 1 hour.

MEXICAN ZUCCHINI

2 tablespoons vegetable oil
1 onion, diced
1 clove garlic, minced
1 pound extra firm tofu, crumbled
3 cups (1 pound) zucchini, chopped
½ cup tomato sauce
4 teaspoons soy sauce
1–2 teaspoons chili powder
1 teaspoon basil
2 tablespoons nutri yeast (optional)

1. Sauté onion and garlic in vegetable oil for 3 minutes.
2. Add tofu, and sauté for another 3 minutes.
3. Add zucchini, and sauté 3 minutes longer.
4. Add remaining ingredients and bring to a boil, then simmer for 3 minutes. May be served by itself or as a taco filling.

SERVES 4–6

TOFU RANCHEROS

1 teaspoon sesame oil
1 leek or onion, diced
2 carrots, diced
2–3 ears of corn, kernels cut off cob
Pinch of cumin, cayenne, or chili powder (optional)
½ pound firm tofu, diced
¼–½ cup salsa
1 tablespoon miso
1 tablespoon arrowroot or cornstarch, dissolved in 1 cup water
⅓ cup scallions, chopped

1. Heat oil in skillet.
2. Sauté cut vegetables 3–5 minutes, adding spices if desired.
3. Stir in tofu.
4. Mix salsa, miso, and dissolved arrowroot in a bowl.
5. Pour sauce over vegetables and tofu. Stir until sauce becomes thick and shiny.
6. Simmer on low heat 10–15 minutes.
7. Add chopped scallions, and serve.

SERVES 4

CELERY BOATS

16 ounces soft tofu
1 tablespoon umeboshi paste
1 tablespoon tahini
1 cup black olives, pitted and chopped
1 bunch celery, trimmed

1. Boil tofu in enough water to cover it for about 1 minute. Drain, retaining cooking water.
2. Blend or mash tofu with umeboshi and tahini until smooth, adding cooking water as needed to make into "dip" consistency.
3. Fold in chopped olives. For best flavor, let mixture sit in refrigerator overnight.
4. Fill grooves of celery with tofu-olive mixture and cut into 2-inch pieces.

STUFFED TOMATOES

SERVES 4

4 large tomatoes
1 pound soft tofu
1 stalk celery, diced
1 small onion, diced
⅓ cup Tofu Mayonnaise (see page 75 for recipe)
2 teaspoons prepared mustard
1 tablespoon miso
1 clove garlic, mashed, or ¼ teaspoon garlic powder
Fresh parsley (as garnish)

1. Hollow out tomatoes and set aside.
2. In a large bowl, mash tofu with a fork; then add celery and onion.
3. In a separate bowl, mix Tofu Mayonnaise, mustard, miso, and garlic.
4. Mix dressing with tofu mixture.
5. Fill tomato shells with mixture, garnish with some fresh parsley, and serve.

STIR-FRIED GREEN BEANS

SERVES 4–6

½ pound green beans, sliced diagonally
1–2 tablespoons oil
1 cup chopped onions
1 cup firm tofu, crumbled
¼ cup unhulled sesame seeds
Sea salt to taste

1. Heat wok. Add oil, and sauté onions until soft.
2. Add tofu, and lightly sauté.
3. Add green beans, cover, and cook 2–3 minutes.
4. Meanwhile, heat skillet or saucepan and toast sesame seeds until they pop.
5. Add sesame seeds to green bean mixture and sprinkle with salt. Serve immediately.

SERVES 3–4

THAI PUMPKIN AND TOFU

1 lemongrass stalk or 1 tablespoon lemongrass powder
1 tablespoon mint, chopped
1 handful fresh coriander, chopped
1 tablespoon lime juice
1 teaspoon Laos powder
1 medium-sized sweet pumpkin, seeded, peeled, and cubed
2 tablespoons nam pla (Siamese seasoning), optional
2 cups coconut milk
1 pound firm tofu, diced

1. Chop and pound lemongrass. Set aside.
2. Mix mint and coriander with lime juice. Set aside.
3. Place lemongrass, Laos, pumpkin, nam pla, and coconut milk in saucepan. Slowly bring mixture to boil while stirring. Simmer until pumpkin is just soft.
4. Add tofu, and stir and simmer until tofu is hot. Turn onto serving plate, and sprinkle with mint mixture.
5. Serve with Thai jasmine rice and blanched greens.

VARIATION

*   Soy milk can be substituted for coconut milk, if desired.

SERVES 4

SWEET POTATO BAKE

1 pound soft tofu
4 medium sweet potatoes or yams, baked or broiled
¼ cup sweetener
2 tablespoons vegetable oil
½ teaspoon salt
1 teaspoon cinnamon
¼ teaspoon nutmeg
⅛ teaspoon ginger

1. Mix all ingredients in blender until smooth.
2. Pour into casserole dish and bake for 20 minutes in preheated oven at 350°F.

STEAMED TOFU À LA VEGETABLES

SERVES 4–6

MARINATED, STEAMED TOFU
½ cup soy sauce
2 tablespoons orange or lemon rind
2 tablespoons corn oil
2 tablespoons rice vinegar
1 tablespoon grated ginger
1 teaspoon grated garlic
2 tablespoons bonita flakes
1 pound firm tofu, pressed and cubed
1 cup brown rice flour
1 teaspoon Japanese lemon pepper
Spinach or cabbage leaves

VEGETABLE SAUCE
3 tablespoons sesame oil
1 cup onion wedges
½ cup sliced shallots
¼ cup sliced celery
½ cup washed bean sprouts
½ cup matchstick carrots
Marinade juice (left from marinating tofu)
1½ cups soup stock
2–3 teaspoons kuzu

GARNISHES
Chopped chives
Grated egg yolk
Sliced scallions

To Marinate and Steam the Tofu:

1. Bring first seven marinade ingredients to a boil.
2. Add tofu to marinade, making sure that tofu is completely covered. Marinate in refrigerator for at least 30 minutes or, better still, overnight. Turn occasionally.
3. Roast flour, lightly roast pepper, and combine the two.
4. Drain marinade from tofu, reserving marinade for use in sauce. Roll tofu in brown rice flour mixture, place on spinach or cabbage leaves, and steam 15–20 minutes. While tofu is steaming, prepare sauce.

To Make the Vegetable Sauce:

1. Heat wok. Add oil, and sauté onions until transparent.
2. Add shallots, and sauté until strong smell disappears.
3. Add the remaining vegetables in order listed, and sauté.
4. Pour in reserved marinade and 1 cup soup stock. Cover and simmer 5 minutes.
5. Dilute kuzu in a few tablespoons cold stock. Stir into vegetables, and keep stirring until sauce thickens, becomes clear, and boils. (Adjust liquid content accordingly.)

To Assemble the Dish:

1. Remove tofu from steamer, and arrange on serving platter. Spoon vegetable sauce on top.
2. Decorate dish with one or all garnishes, and serve.

SERVES 4

CABBAGE WITH TOFU

1 small head cabbage, thinly sliced
3 shiitake mushrooms
1 medium onion, thinly sliced
Water
1 pound firm tofu, cut into ¼-inch cubes
1 tablespoon soy sauce
1 teaspoon umeboshi vinegar
1 teaspoon mirin

1. In a medium-sized saucepan, bring cabbage, shiitake mushrooms, and onion to boil in ½ inch of water.
2. Lower heat, and simmer for about 10 minutes, or until vegetables are soft.
3. While vegetables are simmering, drop tofu cubes into a saucepan of ½ cup boiling water, and boil for 1–2 minutes.
4. Drain tofu cubes and purée them in a food mill, or mash them with a fork or potato masher.
5. Remove shiitake mushrooms from vegetable mixture. Discard tough stems, slice, and return to vegetable mixture.
6. In a large mixing bowl, combine cooked vegetables, mashed tofu, soy sauce, umeboshi vinegar, and mirin.
7. Serve over noodles, garnished with chopped scallions, parsley, toasted sesame seeds, or toasted almonds.

CAULIFLOWER TOFU

SERVES 3–4

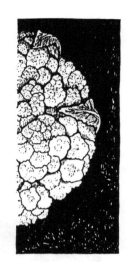

Water
1 tablespoon caraway or dill seed
Sea salt
1 small or ½ large cauliflower, cut into medium-sized pieces
Lemon juice
1 pound soft tofu
4 tablespoons white miso
1 cup soy milk
2 tablespoons mirin

1. Bring water to a boil. Add 1 tablespoon caraway or dill seed, and a pinch of sea salt.
2. Immerse cauliflower in boiling water for 2–3 minutes, depending on thickness of stem. Drain.
3. Arrange cauliflower on a baking tray. Squeeze a little lemon juice on top to prevent discoloration.
4. In blender or food processor, purée tofu, miso, soy milk, and mirin until smooth.
5. Pour tofu mixture over cauliflower, and bake at 350°F for 30 minutes, or until mixture is firm and browned.

SAUTÉED TOFU AND VEGETABLES

SERVES 6

Dark sesame oil
1 cup onions, sliced into half-moons
1 cup fresh sweet corn, removed from the cob
1 cup cabbage, sliced into 1-inch chunks
1 pound firm tofu, crumbled
Sea salt or soy sauce
1 tablespoon sliced scallion (as garnish)

1. Heat a small amount of dark sesame oil in a skillet.
2. Add onions and sauté 1–2 minutes. Stir in corn and cabbage.
3. Sprinkle tofu over the vegetables.
4. Sprinkle 1–2 pinches of sea salt on top, and cover.

5. Reduce flame to medium-low, and cook until vegetables are done and tofu is fluffy. The vegetables are best if they are slightly crisp. During the last 2–3 minutes of cooking, you may season to taste with a little more sea salt or a few sprinkles of soy sauce.
6. Remove and place in a serving bowl. Garnish with scallion slices.

SERVES 3–4

SWEET AND SOUR VEGETABLES

2 teaspoons cornstarch or arrowroot
2 tablespoons water
1 8-ounce can of pineapple chunks
¼ cup water
1 tablespoon vinegar
1 teaspoon sweetener
2 tablespoons soy sauce
¼–½ teaspoon ginger
Dash of pepper
¼ teaspoon salt
2 tablespoons vegetable oil
1 onion, chopped
1 large carrot, thinly sliced
1 green pepper, chopped
1 pound firm tofu, cut in chunks

1. Dissolve cornstarch or arrowroot in 2 tablespoons water.
2. Drain pineapple and save juice.
3. Mix ¼ cup water, ¼ cup pineapple juice, vinegar, sweetener, soy sauce, ginger, a dash of pepper, and salt. Set aside.
4. In a large skillet or wok, sauté onion in vegetable oil for 3 minutes.
5. Add carrot and green pepper, and sauté another 2 minutes.
6. Add tofu to mixture, and continue to cook until tofu is browned.
7. Reduce heat, cover, and simmer until carrots are tender.
8. Add ⅔ cup pineapple chunks to liquid/spice mixture, and stir sauce into tofu mixture.
9. Cook all ingredients while stirring until sauce thickens. Serve alone, or over rice or noodles.

RATATOUILLE WITH TOFU SERVES 4

2 tablespoons olive oil
1 medium onion, chopped
1 clove garlic, minced
½ pound tomatoes, cut up
½ pound firm tofu, cubed
½ teaspoon basil
¼ teaspoon oregano
1 stalk celery, sliced
1 summer squash, sliced
1 green pepper, cut into strips
2 cups eggplant, peeled and cubed

1. Heat oil in a skillet.
2. Sauté the onion and garlic until tender.
3. Add the tomatoes, tofu, basil, and oregano.
4. Turn heat to low, and add the celery, squash, green pepper, and eggplant.
5. Cover skillet and simmer 30 minutes. Serve hot or cold.

TOFU BAKED IN TAHINI-MISO SAUCE SERVES 4

1 pound firm tofu, cut in ½-inch slices
1 tablespoon miso
3 tablespoons tahini
Water
Sliced scallions (as garnish)

1. Stack slices of tofu in a shallow baking dish so that they are slightly tilted and lean against one another.
2. Blend miso and tahini together. Add only enough cold water to make a creamy sauce.
3. Spoon sauce over tofu.
4. Bake in preheated oven at 350°F for 15–20 minutes.
5. Garnish with sliced scallions, and serve.

FRIED TOFU IN MUSHROOM SAUCE

SERVES 4

1 medium egg (optional, add a little more water if desired)
1 tablespoon wheat flour
1 teaspoon water
¼ teaspoon salt
½ pound firm tofu, cut in 1 x 1 x ¼-inch slices
3 tablespoons vegetable oil
¼ pound mushrooms, sliced
2 teaspoons miso, dissolved in 1 cup water
4 teaspoons soy sauce
4 tablespoons cornstarch or arrowroot, dissolved in ¼ cup water

1. To make batter, blend egg, flour, water, and salt until smooth.
2. Dip tofu in batter, and brown in vegetable oil. Set aside.
3. Sauté mushrooms.
4. Add miso to mushrooms, and bring to a boil.
5. Add soy sauce and cornstarch to mushroom mixture, and stir until sauce thickens.
6. Add tofu to sauce, and simmer for 2 minutes before serving.

TOFU, ONIONS, AND MISO

SERVES 4

1 pound firm tofu, cut in ¼-inch slices
2 Spanish onions, cut in 8 wedges
½ teaspoon dark sesame oil
1 teaspoon miso
¼ cup water

1. Brown tofu in a dry cast-iron skillet. Set aside.
2. In a heavy cast-iron or stainless steel pot, sauté onions in toasted sesame oil for 10 minutes.
3. Add tofu to top of onions.
4. Dissolve miso in ¼ cup water, and pour over tofu and onions.
5. Cover, and cook slowly for 40–60 minutes. Serve hot.

MARINATED BAKED TOFU

MAKES 15–20
SLICES

¼ cup soy sauce
¼ cup water
1 teaspoon grated ginger
½ medium onion, diced or grated
1 tablespoon lemon juice
1 pound firm tofu, cut into ¼-inch slices

1. Blend all ingredients except tofu, pour over tofu slices, and marinate in a covered container in the refrigerator for several hours or overnight. This allows the tofu to absorb the flavor of the marinade.
2. Place slices on a 9 x 13-inch baking pan, and pour in remaining marinade. Bake at 350°F for about 30 minutes. Tofu will be dry and chewy. The longer it bakes, the drier the tofu will become.
3. Serve warm as is, mix with noodles or whole grains, or use in sandwiches.

SAUTÉED TOFU IN MISO SAUCE

SERVES 3–4

¼ cup miso
2 tablespoons water
2 teaspoons sake or dry sherry
1 tablespoon sweetener
1 pound extra firm tofu, cut into ½-inch slices
Vegetable oil

1. Prepare sauce by mixing miso, water, sake, and sweetener. Simmer sauce over low heat for 3 minutes.
2. In skillet, sauté tofu slices in vegetable oil.
3. Spread the sauce on the tofu slices, and serve.

SERVES 4

DEEP-FRIED TOFU ROLLS

½ cup carrots, finely diced
½ cup scallions, finely minced
Vegetable oil
Tamari
1 pound firm tofu, drained
Toasted nori seaweed
Sesame or sunflower oil for deep-frying

1. Sauté carrots and scallions in a small amount of oil for 5 minutes.
2. Add a little water to sautéed vegetables, cover, and cook until soft. Then add a little tamari to vegetables, cover, and cook an additional 3 minutes.
3. Remove cover and boil until all water has evaporated.
4. Grind tofu in a suribachi or mortar. Add cooked vegetables to tofu, and mix well.
5. Shape mixture into patties or rolls.
6. Wrap a strip of toasted nori around each patty or roll, pressing firmly so that nori sticks to tofu mixture.
7. Deep-fry rolls in hot oil until golden brown.
8. Drain and serve. These are especially good when served with Tomatofu Dip. (See page 74 for recipe.)

SERVES 4

BASTED PAN-FRIED TOFU

¼ cup soy sauce
1 clove garlic, pressed
1 tablespoon grated ginger or 2 tablespoons ginger juice (optional)
1 pound firm tofu, cut in ½-inch slices

1. Combine soy sauce, garlic, and ginger. Liberally brush mixture over tofu slices.
2. Pan-fry tofu for 5 minutes, or until golden brown on bottom. Turn slices over and repeat process. Serve alone, or as sandwich filling.

MARINATED PAN-FRIED TOFU
SERVES 4–6

3 cups water
½ cup soy sauce
1 teaspoon each of basil, ginger, and curry
Dash of pepper
½ pound firm tofu, cut in ½-inch slices
Vegetable oil

1. In a large bowl, mix together the first four ingredients.
2. Place tofu in marinade, making sure that all slices are submerged. Place the bowl in the refrigerator, and marinate for a few hours, or overnight, turning occasionally.
3. Heat vegetable oil in skillet. When oil is hot, pan-fry tofu until golden brown on both sides. Drain on absorbent paper, and serve.

PAN-FRIED TOFU WITH DAIKON GARNISH
SERVES 5–6

Dark sesame oil
10–12 slices firm tofu, cut into 3 x 2 x ½-inch slices
1 piece ginger, about 2 inches long, grated
Soy sauce
1 piece daikon root, 4–6 inches long, grated

1. Place a small amount of sesame oil in skillet, and pan-fry tofu slices for 2–3 minutes on each side.
2. Place 2 slices of fried tofu on each plate, garnishing each serving with a pinch of grated ginger, a few drops of soy sauce, and a tablespoon of grated daikon.

SERVES 6

BROILED SOY-BASTED TOFU

1 pound firm tofu, sliced into 6 pieces
Soy sauce
Parsley (as garnish)
Sauerkraut (optional)

1. Place tofu slices on baking sheet. Sprinkle a little soy sauce on top of each slice. Broil for 4–5 minutes.
2. Turn tofu slices over, and sprinkle a little soy sauce on second side. Broil for 4–5 additional minutes. Remove.
3. Place one slice of tofu on each individual serving plate. Garnish with a sprig of fresh parsley, and serve. These tofu slices are especially good when served with sauerkraut, which complements the taste of the broiled tofu.

SERVES 6

BROILED TOFU WITH WALNUT-MISO TOPPING

Vegetable oil
1 pound extra firm tofu, cut into ½-inch thick slices
½ cup walnuts, roasted
3 tablespoons miso
3 tablespoons water
1–2 teaspoons mirin (optional)

1. Oil a cookie sheet.
2. Arrange the tofu on the sheet, and broil until golden on both sides.
3. Grind nuts in blender.
4. Add miso, water, and mirin to nuts. Spread mixture on tofu.
5. Broil 1 minute more, and serve.

FRIED WILD RICE WITH TOFU AND VEGETABLES

SERVES 4

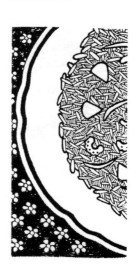

Dark sesame oil
½ cup onions, diced
½ cup celery, diced
1 cup cabbage, cut into 1-inch chunks
4–5 cups cooked wild rice
1 cup firm tofu, crumbled
Tamari soy sauce
1 tablespoon chopped parsley (as garnish)

1. Heat a small amount of dark sesame oil in a skillet.
2. Add onions, and sauté 1–2 minutes.
3. Add celery, cabbage, and wild rice.
4. Place tofu on top of rice mixture.
5. Cover skillet, reduce flame to very low, and simmer until vegetables are tender and tofu is light and fluffy.
6. Add a small amount of tamari soy sauce. Cook 2–3 more minutes. Mix.
7. Place in a serving dish, garnish with chopped parsley, and serve.

SPANISH RICE

SERVES 4

4 tablespoons vegetable oil
1 large onion, diced
1 green pepper, diced
10 ounces firm tofu, crumbled
6 cups rice, cooked
1 pound tomatoes (canned or fresh), chopped
3 teaspoons paprika
4 tablespoons tomato paste

1. Heat vegetable oil in large skillet and sauté onion, green pepper, and tofu until browned.
2. Add remaining ingredients, and mix well.
3. Cover and simmer for 5–10 minutes before serving.

SERVES 4

CHINESE FRIED RICE

1 tablespoon vegetable oil
10 ounces firm tofu, cut in ½-inch cubes
½ cup chopped mushrooms
¼ cup chopped scallions
4 cups cooked rice
1 tablespoon toasted sesame seed oil

1. In skillet, heat 1 tablespoon oil. Add tofu, and sauté over medium heat, stirring frequently but gently to keep the tofu in cubes. Cook until brown. Set aside.
2. In a skillet, pan-fry vegetables over high heat in sesame seed oil, stirring constantly.
3. After 4 minutes, stir rice and tofu into vegetable mixture. Cover, and simmer for another 5 minutes, or until rice and tofu are thoroughly heated.

SERVES 4

FRIED RICE WITH SPROUTS

3 tablespoons vegetable oil
1 onion, minced
1 clove garlic, minced
1 pound firm tofu, cubed
2 stalks celery, sliced
1 cup mushrooms, sliced
½ cup bamboo shoots or mung sprouts
1 cup bok choy (optional)
1 cup peas
2 cups cooked rice
2 tablespoons soy sauce

1. Heat vegetable oil in a large skillet or wok.
2. Add onion, garlic, tofu, celery, mushrooms, bamboo shoots, and peas, and stir-fry for 5 minutes.
3. Add the rice and soy sauce.
4. Cook until rice is heated, and serve.

TOFU CHOW MEIN SERVES 4

3 tablespoons vegetable oil
1 cup onions, chopped
2 cups celery, sliced
1 cup mushrooms, sliced
2 cups mung or soybean sprouts
1 green pepper, diced
1 pound firm tofu, cut into small cubes
½ cup green peas
1 tablespoon arrowroot or cornstarch, dissolved in
1 cup water or vegetable stock
2 tablespoons miso, dissolved in ¼ cup water
2 tablespoons dry sherry
Fried noodles or brown rice

1. In a skillet, heat oil, and stir-fry onions and celery for about 3 minutes.
2. Add mushrooms, mung or soybean sprouts, green pepper, and tofu. Stir-fry for 3 more minutes.
3. In a separate saucepan, heat dissolved arrowroot or cornstarch until thick, stirring constantly.
4. Add miso and dry sherry to sauce.
5. Mix sauce with vegetables, and serve over fried noodles or brown rice.

TOFU-BROCCOLI STIR-FRY SERVES 4

1½ teaspoons arrowroot or cornstarch
¾ cup vegetable stock or water
1 tablespoon dry sherry
2 tablespoons soy sauce
1 teaspoon sesame or vegetable oil
2 quarter-sized slices of fresh ginger, peeled and cut into thin strips
2 cloves garlic, peeled and cut into thin strips
2 heaping cups of broccoli, cut into 2-inch pieces, including stems
1 scallion, cut into 1½-inch thin strips
½ pound firm tofu, cubed

1. Put arrowroot or cornstarch in a cup. Slowly add ¼ cup of cold stock, and mix well. Stir in wine and soy sauce. Set aside.
2. Heat vegetable oil in a wok or frying pan over medium heat. Add ginger and garlic, and stir-fry for 10 seconds.
3. Add broccoli and scallion to ginger mixture, and stir-fry for 1 minute or until broccoli is tender crisp. Remove broccoli and place in bowl.
4. Reduce heat to low, add tofu, and heat.
5. Pour cornstarch or arrowroot mixture over tofu. Mix gently.
6. Add broccoli and stir.
7. Serve as soon as sauce is thick and everything is thoroughly heated.

SERVES 4

TOFU-CABBAGE STIR-FRY

4 tablespoons light sesame oil
3 cloves garlic, crushed, or 1 teaspoon ginger, finely grated
1 medium carrot, cut into matchsticks
1 cup chopped cabbage, washed thoroughly
¼ cup bean sprouts
1 medium mustard cabbage, sliced
¼ cup water
2 tablespoons soy sauce
1 tablespoon kuzu, dissolved in ¼ cup water
1 pound extra firm tofu, cubed

1. Heat oil in a wok. Sauté garlic or ginger briefly, and add carrot, cabbage, and sprouts. Stir-fry over high heat for 2 minutes.
2. Add mustard cabbage and ¼ cup water. Cover. Let sizzle for 1 minute; then stir in soy sauce and tofu. Cover, and simmer over medium heat for 2–3 minutes. Set aside.
3. In separate pot, heat dissolved kuzu, stirring thoroughly. As soon as mixture thickens and starts to clear, stir in vegetables to coat them with the glaze.
4. Simmer for 1 minute, and serve over noodles or rice.

TOFU STIR-FRY WITH WINE

SERVES 4–6

½ cup sake or white wine
3 tablespoons soy sauce
2 teaspoons ginger juice (optional)
1 pound extra firm tofu, cut into 1-inch cubes
2 tablespoons sesame oil
2 cloves garlic, minced
1 onion, thinly sliced
1 red pepper, diced
2 cups broccoli flowerets or sliced Chinese cabbage
1 package (8 ounces) snow peas
¼ cup roasted cashews or almonds

1. In a wok or skillet, bring sake, soy sauce, and ginger to a boil.
2. Add tofu cubes. Cover and simmer for 5 minutes. Remove tofu and broth from wok, and set aside.
3. Heat sesame oil, and stir-fry vegetables over medium-high heat for 3–5 minutes.
4. Stir in remaining broth, tofu, and cashews. Serve warm.

STIR-FRIED TOFU WITH ALMONDS

SERVES 4

4 tablespoons soy sauce
⅛ teaspoon garlic powder
½ teaspoon onion powder
1 tablespoon peanut butter
1 pound firm tofu, cut into 1-inch cubes
2 tablespoons vegetable oil
½ cup red pepper, cut into 1-inch pieces
4 scallions, cut into 1-inch pieces
1 stalk celery, cut into 1-inch pieces
½ cup canned water chestnuts, drained and sliced
½ teaspoon ginger powder or 1½ teaspoons grated fresh ginger
1 cup cold water
1 tablespoon arrowroot or cornstarch
¼ cup roasted almonds

1. Mix together 2 tablespoons soy sauce, garlic powder, onion powder, and peanut butter. Add tofu, and mix well. Refrigerate for 2 hours, stirring occasionally.
2. Heat 1 tablespoon oil in a skillet. Brown tofu on all sides. Remove from pan and set aside.
3. Sauté pepper, scallions, celery, water chestnuts, and ginger until vegetables are crisply tender.
4. Mix together 2 tablespoons soy sauce, water, and arrowroot or cornstarch. Pour mixture over vegetables in the skillet. Stir and simmer until thickened.
5. Add browned tofu and roasted almonds. Mix well, and serve.

SERVES 4–6

SWEET AND SOUR TOFU TOSS

2 cakes firm tofu, cubed
2 tablespoons vegetable oil
8 shallots, sliced
1 pound sliced mushrooms
½ pound honey snap peas, strung
1 cup toasted cashews
Parsley sprigs (as garnish)

MARINADE
¼ cup lemon juice
¼ cup tamari
1 cup water
¼ cup tomato paste
2 tablespoons honey
1 teaspoon minced ginger
4 cloves crushed garlic
Ground black pepper

1. Combine marinade ingredients, and marinate tofu in the mixture for a few hours.
2. Heat oil in a wok and add shallots, mushrooms, and snap peas. Cook for about 3 minutes.
3. Add tofu and marinade to vegetable mixture. Cook for about 15 minutes, and add toasted cashews.
4. Garnish with parsley, and serve with rice.

TOFU BALLS WITH SWEET AND SOUR SAUCE

SERVES 4

TOFU BALLS
1 pound firm tofu
1 tablespoon peanut butter
2 tablespoons parsley, chopped
4 scallions, chopped
½ cup bean sprouts, chopped
½ cup red peppers, chopped
¼ cup fresh mushrooms, sliced
½ cup wheat flour
Vegetable oil for deep-frying
Scallions or shallots, chopped (as garnish)

SWEET AND SOUR SAUCE
½ cup fresh peas
½ cup cooking stock or broth
3 tablespoons oil
4 tablespoons brown rice or whole-wheat flour
½ cup brown rice vinegar
½ cup barley malt, rice syrup, or maltose
½ teaspoon ginger-root juice
2–3 tablespoons shoyu (to taste)
2 teaspoons caraway seeds (crushed)

1. Mash together tofu, peanut butter, parsley, scallions, sprouts, and peppers.
2. Stir in mushrooms, and form mixture into 2-inch balls.
3. Roll balls in flour, and deep-fry until golden brown. Drain.
4. To make sauce, drop peas into boiling stock. Bring once more to boil, and cook uncovered 5 minutes. Drain, and reserve stock.
5. Rinse peas in cold water. Set aside.
6. Heat oil in skillet, and roast flour until fragrant. Heat stock in separate pot, and whisk small amount into flour-oil combination, gradually stirring in more liquid until smooth and creamy.
7. In bowl, combine rest of ingredients, and add to flour mixture. Bring to boil, lower heat, cover, and simmer 10 minutes. Add peas.
8. Serve sauce over tofu balls, and garnish with chopped scallions or shallots.

SERVES 4

Sweet and Sour Dumplings

1 pound firm tofu
1 egg, lightly beaten
1 tablespoon pressed garlic
1 tablespoon grated ginger or orange rind
3 tablespoons minced parsley
½ teaspoon dried oregano
3 cups soup stock
1 teaspoon sea salt
Sweet and Sour Sauce (see recipe on page 113)

1. Mash first six ingredients together.
2. Shape mixture into balls about 1 inch in diameter.
3. Bring 3 cups of stock to boil, add salt, and drop in dumplings.
4. Let stock return to boil, and then add cold water to stop boil. Repeat three times. When balls rise to surface, scoop out and drain.
5. Serve with Sweet and Sour Sauce.

SERVES 4

Filet de Tofu with Apricot Dijon Sauce

1 small onion, chopped
2 cloves garlic, crushed
Vegetable oil
1 tablespoon tamari
1 teaspoon Dijon mustard
2 cups orange juice
1 cup apricot purée or jam
2 pounds extra firm tofu, thinly sliced
Chopped shallots (as garnish)
2 pinches dill (as garnish)

1. Pan-fry onion and garlic in oil. Gradually add tamari, mustard, orange juice, and apricot purée. Stir until you have a smooth sauce.

2. In separate pan, fry tofu in oil, and add to sauce. Cook mixture over low heat until sauce reduces by half.
3. Place tofu in serving dish, and garnish with chopped shallots and dill. Serve with stir-fried vegetables, rice, or a salad.

FRENCH COUNTRY STEW

SERVES 4

Vegetable oil
10 ounces French Country Herb Tofu, cubed
2 onions, cut in wedges
1 medium carrot, cut in ½-inch slices
½ cup string beans
1 medium sweet potato, peeled and cut in ¾-inch slices
½ cup water
½ teaspoon salt
3 tablespoons wheat flour
1 clove garlic, minced
¼ teaspoon Tabasco sauce
1 tablespoon soy sauce
1 package frozen peas

1. Pan-fry tofu in small amount of oil. Set aside.
2. In a 3-quart pot, combine onions, carrot, string beans, potato, ¼ cup water, and salt. Bring to a boil. Then turn heat down and simmer for 25 minutes, or until vegetables are soft and tender.
3. Meanwhile, mix the flour, garlic, Tabasco sauce, soy sauce, and remaining ¼ cup water. Pour flour mixture over vegetables, and continue cooking for another 10 minutes.
4. Add the peas and tofu during the last 5 minutes of cooking, and serve.

FRENCH COUNTRY MUSHROOM SAUCE

SERVES 4

1 tablespoon vegetable oil
¼ cup onions, chopped
½ pound mushrooms, sliced
⅔ cup soy milk or water
⅓ teaspoon salt
⅛ teaspoon black pepper
1 tablespoon arrowroot or cornstarch
10 ounces French Country Herb Tofu, cubed
Brown rice or noodles

1. Sauté onion and mushrooms in oil until brown. Set aside.
2. Mix soy milk, salt, pepper, and arrowroot in separate pot, and bring to a boil, stirring constantly.
3. Stir tofu and mushroom mixture into sauce.
4. Simmer sauce for 3–5 minutes, and serve over brown rice or noodles.

SERVES 2–3

TOFU POLENTA

5 cups water
1 teaspoon salt
1½ cups polenta or cornmeal
½ cup toasted walnuts
½ pound firm tofu
3 tablespoons white miso
1 tablespoon lemon juice

1. Dissolve salt in water and bring to a boil.
2. Pour polenta in, stirring constantly with a whisk, until mixture thickens.
3. Turn heat to low, cover, and simmer 20 minutes, occasionally stirring with a wooden spoon.
4. Pour mixture into a rinsed dish or tray, and leave to set for 2 hours.

5. To make tofu mixture, toast walnuts until oily but not browned.
6. Purée walnuts with remaining ingredients, adding a little water or stock if necessary.
7. Pour tofu mixture over the polenta, and bake for 30 minutes at 350°F. Cut into squares and serve.

TOFU AND TEMPEH BROCHETTES SERVES 3–4

1 cake firm tofu, cut into large cubes
1 block (8 ounces) tempeh, cut into large cubes
2 onions, quartered, layers separated
1 red pepper, cut in squares
1 green pepper, cut in squares

MARINADE
½ cup soy sauce
1 tablespoon garlic, crushed
1 tablespoon ginger, finely grated
2 teaspoons dark sesame oil
2 teaspoons honey or rice malt
2 tablespoons tomato paste
1 tablespoon rice vinegar
1 tablespoon ground coriander
Freshly ground black pepper
½ cup water

1. Arrange tofu and tempeh on skewer, alternating with onions and peppers. Place skewers on flat dish.
2. Bring all marinade ingredients to high heat slowly, and pour mixture over skewers. Marinate for 1 hour.
3. Grill brochettes until well browned, turning occasionally.

TOFU SHISH KEBAB WITH SOY-GINGER GLAZE

SERVES 4

¼ cup soy sauce
1½ teaspoons grated ginger
1 tablespoon rice vinegar
1 tablespoon rice syrup or honey
1 cup water
1 tablespoon mirin
1 pound firm tofu, cut into 1-inch cubes
1 tablespoon kuzu
2 cups broccoli flowerets
2 cups carrot chunks
2 cups turnip wedges
1 tablespoon toasted sesame seeds

1. Bring soy sauce, ginger, rice vinegar, rice syrup, water, and mirin to boil in medium-sized saucepan.
2. Add tofu cubes, lower heat, and simmer for 15 minutes. Remove tofu and set aside. Allow soy sauce mixture to cool.
3. Dissolve kuzu in a small amount of cool soy sauce mixture, and stir it back into that mixture.
4. Stir soy sauce mixture over medium heat for about 5 minutes, until thickened and clear, and set aside.
5. Steam broccoli, carrots, and turnips until they are lightly cooked, but still firm, and set aside.
6. Skewer tofu and vegetables on stainless steel or bamboo skewers, alternating tofu with vegetables so that each skewer looks attractive and colorful.
7. Spoon soy sauce-kuzu sauce over each skewer and broil for a few minutes, until hot and glazed with sauce.
8. Remove from broiler, sprinkle with toasted sesame seeds, and serve with rice, if desired.

SHISH KEBAB
WITH MUSTARD MARINADE

SERVES 4–6

2½ pounds firm tofu, cut in 1-inch cubes
Vegetable oil (optional)
12 tomato or eggplant wedges
12 mushrooms, halved
12 sweet pepper chunks
6 green pepper chunks

MARINADE
3 tablespoons prepared mustard
4 tablespoons sake or white wine
2 tablespoons vinegar
4 tablespoons vegetable oil
2 tablespoons maple syrup
1 teaspoon dry rosemary
1 teaspoon dry oregano
2 cloves garlic, minced
2 teaspoons minced ginger root
1–2 teaspoons sea salt or 3–4 tablespoons shoyu (to taste)

1. Deep-fry tofu cubes in oil, or use as is.
2. Combine the marinade ingredients in a bowl, add the tofu cubes, and then add the vegetables. Toss lightly so that all the vegetables are coated with the marinade. Allow to marinate for 1 hour, occasionally turning the tofu and vegetables. After 1 hour, drain off the marinade, and reserve for later use.
3. If using bamboo skewers, soak the skewers in cold water, and then drain. Stainless steel skewers may also be used.
4. Place the tofu cubes on the skewers, alternating with the vegetables to form a colorful arrangement.
5. Cook over a grill until brown and fragrant, occasionally basting the vegetables with the reserved marinade. Serve hot, alone or over rice.

SERVES 4

GINGER TOFU PIE

1 cup uncooked brown rice
1½ cups water with a pinch of sea salt
4 medium carrots, grated
2 medium turnips, grated
1 medium onion, chopped
1 cup water
½ teaspoon sea salt
½ pound firm tofu
1 small onion, diced
1 teaspoon grated ginger
1 tablespoon soy sauce
1 small bunch parsley, chopped
1 teaspoon light or dark sesame oil
1 tablespoon toasted sesame seeds

1. Pressure-cook or boil rice, water, and sea salt until all water has been absorbed.
2. While rice is cooking, bring carrots, turnips, medium onion, and ¼ teaspoon sea salt to a boil in ½ cup water.
3. Lower heat, and simmer for 10 minutes, or until vegetables are soft. Set aside.
4. Boil tofu, onion, ginger, soy sauce, and ½ cup water over medium heat for about 5 minutes.
5. Purée tofu mixture in a food mill placed over a large bowl.
6. Put 1 cup of rice through the food mill placed over the same bowl. Not all of the grains will go through.
7. Combine tofu mixture, whole and partially puréed rice, and parsley.
8. Moisten your hands with water and form a crust, using your hands to mold the mixture onto a 9-inch pie plate.
9. Brush crust with oil, and put under broiler for 5 minutes.
10. Remove from broiler, and fill crust with carrot, turnip, and onion mixture.
11. Sprinkle sesame seeds over filling, and bake at 350°F for 15 minutes. Serve hot.

ZUCCHINI TOFU PIE

SERVES 8

4 cups zucchini, thinly sliced
1 cup onions, chopped
¼ cup olive oil
1 pound firm tofu
¼ cup parsley, chopped
1 clove garlic or ¼ teaspoon garlic powder
½ teaspoon oregano
½ teaspoon basil
1 teaspoon salt
2 eggs (optional)
1 cup shredded mozzarella cheese (optional)
9-inch pie crust

1. Sauté zucchini and onions in oil until tender. Set aside.
2. Mix tofu, parsley, garlic, oregano, basil, salt, and eggs in blender until smooth.
3. In bowl, combine tofu mixture with vegetables and shredded cheese.
4. Pour mixture into pie crust.
5. Bake 40 minutes in preheated oven at 375°F. Serve hot or cold.

SPINACH PIE

SERVES 6

10-inch pie crust (double, if you wish to use a top crust)
10 ounces fresh or frozen spinach (may substitute broccoli), chopped
1 pound firm tofu
1 teaspoon salt
⅛ teaspoon nutmeg
⅛ teaspoon pepper
Small clove garlic
1½ cups grated Cheddar cheese (optional)

1. Prepare pie crusts; bake lower crust in preheated oven at 350°F.

2. Briefly steam spinach or broccoli.
3. In a blender, mix tofu, salt, nutmeg, pepper, and garlic until smooth.
4. In a bowl, mix spinach, tofu mixture, and cheese.
5. Pour mixture into pie crust, and, if desired, cover with upper crust. For double-crust pie, bake at 450°F for 10 minutes, then at 350°F for another 45 minutes. For single-crust pie, bake at 350°F for 40 minutes. Serve hot or cold.

SERVES 6–8

TOFU-BROCCOLI PIE

2 tablespoons tahini
3 tablespoons soy sauce
½ teaspoon sea salt
2 pounds soft tofu, mashed
1 tablespoon kuzu or arrowroot powder
¼ cup water
1 pound broccoli, chopped
1 prebaked pie shell

1. Combine soy sauce, tahini, salt, and tofu in a bowl.
2. Dilute kuzu or arrowroot in ¼ cup water and, in a saucepan, combine with the first mixture. Simmer over medium-low heat for 7–10 minutes.
3. Steam broccoli until almost tender.
4. Add broccoli to tofu mixture, and spoon carefully into baked pie shell.
5. Bake in preheated oven at 300°F for 8–10 minutes to blend flavors.
6. Let cool for 30–60 minutes before serving.

TOFU TARTS OR FLAN

SERVES 4–6

PASTRY
4 cups whole-meal flour
Pinch sea salt
½ cup oil (increase this to
¾ cup for "shorter" pastry, and reduce water)
1⅓–1½ cups water (depending on flour)

WALNUT-SPINACH FILLING
2 tablespoons olive oil
3 cloves garlic, crushed
3 onions, chopped
1 tablespoon coriander powder
3 tablespoons soy sauce
2 teaspoons oregano
Dash of freshly grated nutmeg
1 cup cooked rice or millet
1 cup walnuts, chopped
1 bunch spinach, chopped and blanched

TOFU MIXTURE
½ pound firm tofu
1 tablespoon white miso
1 tablespoon mirin
2–3 tablespoons liquid reserved from walnut-spinach sauté

To Make the Pastry:

1. Add salt to flour, and gradually add oil until well mixed.
2. Add water, beginning with 1 cup, and adding more as needed.
3. Mix with a wooden spoon until the mixture clings together. Then mix with hands to form a dough. The mixture must be pliable, not hard, so add more water if necessary (whole-meal grains vary a lot in their capacity to absorb water).

4. Knead dough for 1 minute. This dough can be used immediately, or can be kept sealed for 3 days, after which time it will become sourdough and much lighter, with a pleasant tang. Use either tart tins with removable bases or one large flan tray. Oil tins, roll out the pastry, and line the tins with the pastry. Set aside.

To Make the Walnut-Spinach Filling:

1. Heat oil; sauté garlic and onions for 2 minutes.
2. Add remaining ingredients except walnuts and spinach. Sauté 2–3 minutes..
3. Add spinach and walnuts; mix well.
4. Drain and reserve liquid for use in tofu mixture.

To Assemble the Tarts:

1. Purée all tofu mixture ingredients until smooth.
2. Place spinach filling in pastry shells.
3. Spoon on tofu mixture, and smooth with spatula.
4. Bake in preheated oven at 400°F for 15 minutes or until the tofu sets and is browned. Grill under broiler, if desired, and serve.

SERVES 6–8

QUICHE NELSON

1½ pounds soft tofu
3 tablespoons sesame tahini
2 tablespoons soy sauce
1 teaspoon sea salt
½ cup water
2 medium-sized onions, grated
Small bunch parsley, chopped
1 prebaked pie shell

1. In a suribachi or blender, mix tofu, sesame tahini, soy sauce, sea salt, and water until creamy.
2. Add onions and parsley to mixture, combining well.
3. Pour filling into crust, smoothing top with a spatula.
4. Bake for 45 minutes at 350°F. To test if done, insert toothpick into the center. When toothpick comes out dry, quiche is ready.

SCRAMBLED TOFU WITH MUSHROOMS AND PEPPERS

SERVES 4

1 medium onion, diced
1 teaspoon light or dark sesame oil
8 medium mushrooms, sliced
½ green or red pepper, diced
¼ teaspoon sea salt
1 pound soft tofu
¼ teaspoon tumeric

1. Sauté onion in oil in a medium-sized frying pan.
2. Add mushrooms, green or red pepper, and sea salt.
3. Sauté until pepper is tender.
4. Add tofu, mashing it with a wooden spoon to break it into small pieces. Continue to sauté for 5–8 minutes, stirring in tumeric as it cooks.
5. Serve tofu hot with toast, muffins, or rice cakes.

SCRAMBLED TOFU AND CORN

SERVES 4–6

2 tablespoons water
2 pounds soft tofu, crumbled
3 cups fresh sweet corn, removed from cob
Sea salt
¼ cup sliced scallions

1. Heat 2 tablespoons of water in a pot and add tofu. Place sweet corn on top of tofu, and sprinkle a little sea salt on top of corn. Cover, and cook over a low flame for 3–4 minutes. Do not overcook.
2. Mix in scallions after tofu has cooled sufficiently; this ensures that the scallions will not lose their bright green color. Garnish with additional scallion slices, and serve.

SERVES 4

VEGETABLE-TOFU SCRAMBLE

2 tablespoons vegetable oil
1 onion, diced
½ cup red pepper, diced
1 carrot, grated
1 celery stalk, diced
1 pound soft tofu
¼–½ teaspoon salt
¼ teaspoon onion powder
¼ teaspoon garlic powder
¼ cup parsley or scallions, chopped (as garnish)

1. Sauté vegetables in oil for 3–5 minutes. Set aside.
2. Combine tofu with spices. Add to vegetables. Cover and simmer for 5 minutes, stirring occasionally.
3. Garnish with parsley or scallions, and serve.

SERVES 6–8

SCRAMBLED TOFU SATORI

2 cloves garlic, chopped
½ teaspoon grated ginger
3 teaspoons sesame or olive oil
1 medium onion, diced
1 medium green pepper, diced
1 medium carrot, diced
Pinch sea salt
3 pounds firm tofu
¼ teaspoon tumeric
Soy sauce or sea salt to taste

1. Sauté garlic and ginger in lightly oiled skillet.
2. Add onion, green pepper, and carrot to hot skillet, along with a pinch of sea salt. Sauté until vegetables are soft.
3. Mash the 3 pounds of drained tofu in skillet, using fork or potato masher. Cook over high flame for 5–7 minutes.
4. Stir in tumeric. Before serving, add soy sauce or sea salt to taste.

ONION AND TOMATO PIZZA

SERVES 4

CRUST (Double recipe)
½ cup tepid water
1 tablespoon dry yeast
½ cup whole-wheat flour
1 teaspoon sea salt
2½ cups whole-wheat flour
Water to form dough
Cornmeal for base of pizza

TOPPING
3 tablespoons diced ginger
4 cups sliced onions
1 cup water
½ cup soy sauce (to taste)
24 quartered tomatoes (6 cups)
Sea salt to taste
3 tablespoons olive oil
2 tablespoons chopped garlic
2 tablespoons oregano
1 teaspoon dried basil or 1 tablespoon fresh basil
1–2 tablespoons sea salt
2 tablespoons vegetable oil
2½ pounds firm tofu, mashed or broken into pieces
1 cup sliced pickled mushrooms
Minced parsley
½ cup sliced olives

To Make the Crust:

1. Combine water and yeast. Stir until smooth.
2. Stir in the ½ cup flour, cover, and set aside in a warm place until mixture bubbles (5–10 minutes).
3. Beat mixture down and add the rest of the ingredients, except for the cornmeal, using only enough water to form a smooth elastic dough.
4. Knead several minutes.
5. Preheat the oven to 375°F.
6. Warm oiled pizza tray and sprinkle cornmeal over the oiled tray.

7. Divide the dough in half. Wrap one half, and freeze for future use.
8. Shape the remaining half into a circle with your hands.
9. Place dough on tray, oil fingers, and press fingers into the dough, shaping it into a large circle to fit the tray.
10. Cover, and set aside until the dough doubles in size. Bake 20–25 minutes.

To Make the Topping:

1. Place ginger in pan. Cover with onions, water, and soy sauce.
2. Bring ginger mixture to a boil, cover, and simmer 5 minutes. Remove cover, and reduce until dry. Set aside.
3. Place tomatoes in a large pot, and bring to a boil.
4. Add a pinch of salt to tomatoes, lower heat, and simmer covered until tender (10–15 minutes).
5. Strain off juice, and press solids through a sieve. Discard the skin and seeds.
6. Heat skillet, add oil, and sauté garlic. Then add oregano, basil, tomato mixture, and salt, and bring to a boil.
7. Cook without a lid until reduced by one-third, or until desired consistency is reached. Set aside.
8. Heat skillet, add oil, and sauté tofu, sprinkling with salt to taste.

To Assemble the Pizza:

1. Place onions on top of crust, and alternate with tomato sauce.
2. Cover with pickled mushrooms and tofu.
3. Sprinkle with parsley, and place olives around the edges.
4. Reheat in oven just before serving.

MY FAVORITE MUFFIN PIZZAS

SERVES 4

TOFU-RICE TOPPING
2 cups leftover rice or soft rice (pressed into measuring cup)
¼ pound soft tofu
1 large or 2 small umeboshi plums (pits removed)
½ small onion, chopped
Water to achieve "cheesy" consistency
(will vary depending on how moist the rice is)

SAUCE
2 cloves garlic, minced
½ small onion, finely chopped
½ green pepper, finely chopped
1 teaspoon olive oil
¼ teaspoon basil
Pinch cayenne pepper
6 ounces tomato paste
½ cup water
¼ teaspoon dark miso

GARNISHES
Green or black olives, sliced
Cooked tempeh, tofu, or seitan pieces
Mushrooms, sliced
Onions, sliced
Green pepper, sliced

4 whole-wheat English muffins, sliced in half

1. Purée tofu-rice topping ingredients in a blender, food processor, or suribachi, adding enough water to achieve a melted-cheese-like consistency. Set mixture aside.
2. To make sauce, sauté garlic, onion, and green pepper in olive oil in a medium-sized saucepan. Add basil, cayenne pepper, tomato paste, and water. Bring to boil, lower heat, and simmer for 10 minutes, or until vegetables are very soft.
3. Turn off heat, stir in miso, and set aside.

4. To assemble pizzas, place 8 muffin halves on baking sheet in preheated oven at 400°F for 15 minutes, or until lightly toasted.

5. Remove muffins from oven, and top each one with a heaping tablespoon of sauce, a heaping tablespoon of tofu-rice topping, and any of the garnishes you desire.

6. Return muffin pizzas to oven, and bake for 15 minutes, or until pizzas are hot and bubbly.

CRUSTY MILLET PIZZA WITH CARROT SAUCE

SERVES 4

TOFU MIXTURE
1 cup sweet rice, soaked overnight in 2 cups water
Pinch sea salt
½ pound firm tofu
1 medium onion, finely chopped
2 small umeboshi plums with pits removed
or 1 heaping teaspoon umeboshi plum paste
Water

CRUST
1 cup uncooked millet
2½ cups water
⅛ teaspoon sea salt
1 teaspoon olive oil

SAUCE
4 large carrots or 6 medium carrots, sliced
1 large onion, chopped
1 teaspoon umeboshi plum paste
2 cloves garlic, minced
¼ teaspoon basil
¼ teaspoon ground bay leaf
¼–½ cup water
1 teaspoon miso

To Make the Tofu Mixture:

1. Pressure-cook rice, soaking water, pinch sea salt, and whole piece of tofu for 20 minutes.

2. Stir hot rice-tofu mixture, onion, and umeboshi in suribachi with a surikogi (pestle) until most of the grains are mashed, and the mixture is sticky.
3. Add ¼–½ cup water, and stir a few more minutes to achieve a thinner, more melted-cheese-like consistency.
4. Let this mixture sit overnight. It should be lightly covered so that air can get to it. It can also be prepared in the morning and used that evening, but once used, it must be refrigerated.

To Make the Crust:

1. Bring millet, water, and sea salt to boil in medium-sized saucepan.
2. Lower heat, cover, and simmer for 30 minutes.
3. Press warm mixture onto a round 12-inch pizza pan. A 9 x 12-inch rectangular baking sheet can also be used.
4. Brush millet crust with olive oil, and put under broiler for 3–5 minutes, or until light golden brown. Remove from broiler, and set aside.

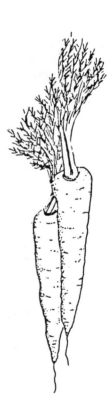

To Make the Sauce:

1. Bring all sauce ingredients except for miso to a boil.
2. Lower heat, cover, and simmer for about 20 minutes, or until carrots are very soft.
3. Purée all ingredients, including miso, in a food mill. The sauce should have the consistency of thick mayonnaise.

To Assemble the Pizza:

1. Spread sauce on top of crust, and spread tofu mixture on top of sauce.
2. If you like, add a topping of your choice, such as raw scallions, sautéed or raw onions, olives, cooked tempeh, seitan, or steamed squash.
3. Bake for 15 minutes at 400°F, or put under broiler for about 5 minutes to brown the top. Serve warm.

TOFU SPINACH CASSEROLE

SERVES 6

2 pounds soft tofu
1½ cups raw whole almonds
3 tablespoons soy sauce
1 cup water
3 cloves garlic
1 quart mushrooms, sliced
2 cups onions, diced into ¾-inch pieces
2 tablespoons oil
⅓ cup tamari
1 teaspoon sea salt
2 tablespoons thyme
2 tablespoons basil
½ teaspoon pepper
1½ quarts fresh spinach, chopped
Sesame seeds

1. Place tofu in a colander and allow to drain.
2. Spread almonds on a cookie sheet and bake at 375°F for 10–12 minutes, until the interior is lightly browned and crunchy.
3. Toss almonds with 3 tablespoons soy sauce immediately after removing from oven.
4. Allow almonds to cool. When cool, purée with water and garlic in food processor (small almond chunks are okay).
5. Sauté mushrooms and onions in oil until mushrooms release some of their water (approximately 10 minutes).
6. Add soy sauce and seasonings to mushroom mixture, and cook over a very low flame another 10 minutes. Let cool.
7. Crumble drained tofu (tofu must be well-drained to reach desired consistency), and combine with all ingredients, except sesame seeds, in large bowl.
8. Spoon mixture into oiled individual casseroles. Sprinkle generously with sesame seeds.
9. Bake in preheated oven at 400°F for 12–15 minutes. Note that flavor will be greatly enhanced if you use fresh herbs. Texture should be firm and moist, not crumbly. If individual casseroles are not available, bake in large baking dish at 350°F for 20–30 minutes, or until hot in the center.

HOT TOFU SANDWICH

SERVES 1

1 large slice of tofu, about ½ inch thick
2 teaspoons miso
2 tablespoons tahini
1 tablespoon nutritional yeast
2 tablespoons hot water
1 clove garlic, pressed (optional)
1 thick slice of whole grain bread
Chopped parsley (as garnish)

1. Place tofu under broiler of toaster oven or regular oven, and broil until brown. Turn tofu over, and brown second side.
2. While tofu is cooking, mix together miso, tahini, and yeast. Slowly stir in enough hot water to make a sauce. Stir in garlic, if desired.
3. Place bread under broiler, and toast both sides.
4. Place bread on plate, and top with hot tofu. Pour sauce over sandwich, and garnish with chopped parsley. Serve with green salad.

FRIED TOFU SANDWICHES WITH SAUERKRAUT

SERVES 4–6

Dark sesame oil
1 pound firm tofu, cut into 8 or 10 slices
Soy sauce
8 or 10 slices whole-wheat sourdough
½ cup sauerkraut

1. Heat a small amount of dark sesame oil in a skillet.
2. Place tofu slices in skillet, with a couple of drops of soy sauce on each slice.

3. Fry on one side 2–3 minutes. Turn slices over, place 1 or 2 drops of soy sauce on this side, and fry for 2–3 minutes. Turn over once again, and fry 1 minute more. Remove.
4. Make each sandwich by placing 2 slices of fried tofu side by side on a slice of bread, with 1–2 tablespoons of sauerkraut on top. Cover with another slice of bread.
5. Slice sandwiches in half, and serve.

SERVES 4–6

TOFU BURGERS

½ onion, minced
½ green or sweet red pepper, minced
1 stalk celery, minced
2 tablespoons vegetable oil
1 pound extra firm tofu, mashed
2 tablespoons wheat flour
2 tablespoons soy sauce
2 eggs, beaten (optional)
¼ cup grated Cheddar cheese (optional)
Bread crumbs (optional)
Ketchup or mustard (optional)

1. In skillet, sauté onion, green or red pepper, and celery in vegetable oil.
2. In bowl, combine vegetable mixture with tofu, flour, soy sauce, eggs, and cheese.
3. Shape into patties. The more mixture in each patty, the better its shape will be retained during cooking.
4. Dip each patty in bread crumbs, if desired, and brown in oiled skillet or bake in preheated oven at 350°F for 30 minutes.
5. Serve hot, with ketchup or mustard.

ALFALFA-ALMOND POCKET BREAD SURPRISES

SERVES 4

1 pound firm tofu
4 tablespoons miso
4 tablespoons almond butter
1 tablespoon grated orange rind
2 teaspoons mustard
1 cup alfalfa sprouts
1 cup grated carrots
¼ cup grated cabbage
4 pita bread pockets

1. Cream tofu, miso, butter, orange rind, and mustard together.
2. Mix in the sprouts, carrots, and cabbage.
3. Cut open bread, stuff with filling, and serve.

TOFU GRILLED "CHEESY" SANDWICHES

MAKES 2
SANDWICHES

1 small onion, diced
½ teaspoon light sesame oil
¼ pound firm tofu, crumbled
1 piece mochi, 2 inches square and ½-inch high,
cut into very small pieces or grated
2 tablespoons water
1 teaspoon umeboshi plum paste
⅛ teaspoon tumeric
1 teaspoon prepared mustard
4 slices sourdough bread
Oil to brush pan for grilling sandwiches

1. Sauté onion in oil for a few minutes until pearly white.
2. Add tofu, mochi, and water, and sauté for a few minutes more.

3. Add umeboshi plum paste, tumeric, and mustard to mochi mixture. Stir continuously for 1–2 minutes, until mixture becomes sticky..
4. Remove mochi mixture from heat, and spread evenly on 2 slices of bread. Then top each with another slice of bread.
5. Grill sandwiches on a lightly oiled pan over medium heat for about 5 minutes on each side, until each side is toasted. Slice, and serve hot.

VARIATIONS

- After spreading bread with mochi mixture, add sliced pickles, top with the other slice of bread, and grill.
- Put mochi mixture in a blender for a creamier texture.
- Add 1 tablespoon tahini to mochi mixture for a richer taste.

SERVES 4

TOFU SLOPPY JOES

2 tablespoons vegetable oil
1 large onion, finely chopped
1 pound firm tofu, crumbled
1 clove garlic, minced, or ¼ teaspoon garlic powder
1 teaspoon oregano
1 teaspoon basil
1 cup spaghetti sauce
4 hamburger buns or English muffins
Parmesan, mozzarella, or other cheese of your choice, grated

1. In a skillet, heat oil, and sauté onion and tofu over medium heat until onions have browned.
2. Add garlic, oregano, and basil, and simmer until liquid has evaporated. Then, stir in spaghetti sauce.
3. In a baking pan, spread opened hamburger buns. Place buns in 350°F oven, and toast lightly.
4. Remove buns from oven, spread with sauce, and sprinkle with cheese.
5. Return buns to oven and heat until cheese melts. Serve immediately.

WALNUT BALLS IN CREAM SAUCE　　SERVES 4–6

WALNUT BALLS
1 egg (optional)
3 tablespoons whole-wheat bread crumbs
2 tablespoons brown rice, corn barley, or whole-wheat flour
2 tablespoons kuzu or arrowroot flour
1 teaspoon dried basil
½ teaspoon dried thyme
1 teaspoon dried oregano
2 tablespoons miso or 1 teaspoon sea salt
2½ pounds firm tofu, pressed and mashed
¼ cup walnuts, chopped
3 tablespoons onions, minced
¼ cup parsley, chopped
Oil for deep-frying

SAUCE BECHAMEL
2 tablespoons brown rice or whole-wheat flour
2 teaspoons oil
½ cup chopped onion
¼ cup chopped celery or watercress
½ cup chopped scallions
1 tablespoon sesame tahini
1 teaspoon sea salt to taste
2 cups fish, chicken, or vegetable stock

To Make the Walnut Balls:

1. Beat the egg, and add the bread crumbs, flour, kuzu, herbs, and salt or miso.
2. Combine bread-crumb mixture with tofu, walnuts, onions, and parsley, blending well.
3. Shape into little balls.
4. Heat oil, and deep-fry walnut balls until golden. Drain.

To Make the Sauce:

1. Lightly roast the flour until it begins to smell nutty. Set aside.
2. Heat skillet, add oil, and sauté onion, celery, and scallions until they become transparent.

3. Add flour, tahini, salt, and stock.
4. Cream the soup in blender or food processor.
5. Return soup to pot, bring to boil, cover, and simmer with the lid ajar for 10 minutes.
6. Taste and adjust seasonings before serving.

To Assemble the Dish:

1. Preheat oven to 350°F.
2. Place walnut balls in oiled casserole dish, cover with Sauce Bechamel, and bake 15 minutes or until warm. Serve.

SERVES 4–6   # *TOFU CRABMEAT OMELET*

½ pound firm tofu, drained and mashed
5–6 mushrooms, finely sliced
½ pound crabmeat, finely chopped
1 teaspoon mirin or cooking sherry
½ teaspoon tamari or soy sauce
1 tablespoon peas (frozen or fresh)
1 teaspoon whole-meal flour, sifted
4 eggs, lightly beaten
1 teaspoon butter
1 teaspoon vegetable oil
Dash of tamari (as garnish)
Grated daikon (as garnish)

1. Combine all ingredients except butter, oil, and garnishes, mixing well.
2. Heat butter and oil in a large pan.
3. Pour in half the mixture and cover.
4. Cook over a low heat for about 15 minutes, or until all the egg has set. Transfer to heated plate, and keep warm.
5. Repeat cooking process with the rest of the egg mixture.
6. Slice cooked omelets into 1 x 2-inch bars.
7. Serve hot with a little extra tamari and grated daikon (hot radish).

TREASURE TRIANGLES

SERVES 6–8

TOFU TRIANGLES
4 cakes extra firm tofu, ½ pound each
Arrowroot flour or bread crumbs
Oil for deep-frying

MAYONNAISE CURRY
Leftover tofu after making pockets
3 tablespoons lemon juice
4 tablespoons oil
¼ cup brown rice vinegar
1 teaspoon curry powder or tumeric
½ teaspoon sea salt
4 tablespoons minced parsley
4 tablespoons minced carrots or red pepper

SALAD FILLING
2 cups thinly sliced radishes
⅓ cup olives, pitted and cut lengthwise into thin strips
1 tablespoon tahini
4 tablespoons chopped spring onions
4–6 lettuce leaves, torn

To Make the Tofu Triangles:

1. Press tofu 15 minutes with a heavy object.
2. Cut diagonally into triangles.
3. Roll in arrowroot or bread crumbs.
4. Heat oil in skillet, and deep-fry the triangles until lightly browned. Drain.
5. When triangles are cool, scoop out centers with melon baller. Save the scooped-out tofu for the Mayonnaise Curry.

To Make the Mayonnaise Curry:

1. Blend the curry ingredients, except parsley and carrots, until smooth and creamy.
2. Stir in carrots and parsley.

To Assemble the Triangles:

1. Mix salad filling ingredients together, and toss with Mayonnaise Curry.
2. Fill the triangles with the salad, and serve.

SERVES 4–6

TOFU STROGANOFF

½ pound extra firm tofu, cut into 1-inch cubes
Oil
1 cup chopped onions or shallots
½ pound fresh mushrooms (4 cups), quartered,
or 2 cups dried mushrooms
1 teaspoon dried oregano or 2 tablespoons fresh oregano, chopped
1 cup sliced green beans
¼ cup mirin
1 cup yogurt

MARINADE
¼ cup oil
½ cup shoyu
½ teaspoon garlic
1 teaspoon cumin or 5 spice powder
¼ teaspoon pepper
¼ cup water to cover

1. In large bowl, combine the marinade ingredients. Stir in tofu, and marinate for at least 30 minutes.
2. Heat skillet; add oil, and sauté onions 2–3 minutes, or until transparent.
3. Add mushrooms and lightly sauté.
4. Add tofu and oregano. Cover, and cook 5 minutes.
5. Blanch green beans in salted water. Drain, rinse in cold water, and add to tofu mixture.
6. When mushrooms are tender, stir in mirin and yogurt, and serve.

CORN FRITTERS

SERVES 6–8

FRITTERS
1 cup stock, water, or soy milk
1 cup whole-wheat flour
2 cups fresh corn kernels, crushed
1 cup onion, minced
½ cup parsley, minced
½ teaspoon sea salt
Vegetable oil

RUSSIAN SAUCE
½ pound soft tofu
2 tablespoons tahini or 1 tablespoon sesame oil
2 tablespoons lemon juice
1 tablespoon rice vinegar
1 teaspoon sea salt
1 teaspoon hot mustard or grated garlic
1 hard-boiled egg (optional)
3 tablespoons diced onions
1 cup minced olives
3 tablespoons minced parsley

To Make the Fritters:

1. Combine the stock, water, or soy milk with the flour. Mix to form a paste.
2. Stir in remaining ingredients, except for oil.
3. Heat oil in pan, and drop batter by spoonfuls into oil.
4. Fry until lightly brown, and serve with Russian Sauce.

To Make the Sauce:

1. Drop tofu into boiling water, and boil for 1–2 minutes.
2. Drain tofu, and combine with the next six ingredients. Blend until creamy and smooth.
3. Mix in onions, olives, and parsley, and serve over fritters.

SERVES 4–6

HIZIKI WITH FRIED TOFU

1 cup firm tofu, sliced in 1-inch cubes or 2-inch-long rectangles
Light sesame oil
1 cup onions, cut in half-moons
1 cup carrots, cut in matchsticks
1 ounce hiziki, washed, soaked 3–5 minutes
(about 1½–2 cups soaked), and sliced
Water and hiziki soaking water (if not too salty)
Soy sauce

1. Deep-fry cubed or sliced tofu in light sesame oil until golden brown. Place on paper towels to drain excess oil.
2. Place drained tofu slices in pot. Add onions, carrots, and hiziki, with hiziki on top.
3. Add water to cover fried tofu and vegetables, but not hiziki. Add a small amount of soy sauce, and bring to a boil. Cover, reduce flame to low, and simmer for about 45 minutes.
4. Add a little more soy sauce for a mild salty taste, and simmer until almost all remaining liquid is gone.
5. Mix and serve.

SERVES 6

FISH-STUFFED TOFU

1 scallion, minced
½ pound fish fillets
1 pound fresh abalone, trimmed
White pepper (optional)
3½ pounds firm tofu, drained and patted dry

1. Grind or process scallion together with fish and abalone. Add a little white pepper if desired. Form mixture into 12 balls to fill 12 triangles.
2. Cut each tofu cake in half lengthwise, and then into triangles. On the diagonal cut, make a slit in the face to accommodate filling, but don't cut through the triangle.
3. Carefully insert one fish ball into each slit, flattening to fit.
4. Heat oil, and deep-fry until golden. Serve with chili sauce.

DRIED TOFU, CARROTS, AND ONIONS

SERVES 4

Dark sesame oil
1 cup onions, sliced in half-moons
1 cup dried firm tofu, soaked and sliced
1 cup carrots, cut into matchsticks
Water
Soy sauce

1. Heat a small amount of sesame oil in a skillet. Add onions, and sauté 1–2 minutes.
2. Add tofu, and sauté 1–2 minutes.
3. Add carrots and enough water to cover bottom of skillet. Bring to a boil.
4. Stir in a small amount of soy sauce, lower flame, and cover. Simmer several minutes, until carrots and onions are tender.
5. Season with a little soy sauce, stir, and sauté until all liquid is gone. Serve.

KIMPIRA BURDOCK, CARROTS, AND DRIED TOFU

SERVES 3–4

1 cup dried firm tofu
Dark sesame oil
1 cup burdock, shaved or cut into matchsticks
2 cups carrots, cut into matchsticks
Water
Soy sauce

1. Place dried tofu in warm or hot water and soak for 3–4 minutes. Rinse in cold water. Remove, squeeze out water, and slice into rectangles.
2. Heat a small amount of dark sesame oil in a skillet. Add burdock and sauté for 2–3 minutes.

3. Add carrots and dried tofu, and sauté 2–3 minutes.
4. Place a small amount of water in the skillet, covering the vegetables about halfway.
5. Add a small amount of soy sauce, and bring to a boil. Reduce flame to low, cover, and simmer for about 30 minutes, or until liquid is gone, and serve.

VARIATIONS

- If you wish to avoid using oil, omit sautéing, and boil all ingredients instead.
- For a different flavor, use fresh sliced lotus root instead of burdock.
- Try using tempeh or fresh tofu instead of dried tofu.

BOILED TOFU WITH GINGER-PARSLEY SAUCE

SERVES 6

¼ cup water
1 pound firm tofu, sliced into 6 pieces
½ cup water
1–1½ tablespoons soy sauce
¼ teaspoon fresh grated ginger
1 tablespoon fresh minced parsley (as garnish)

1. Place about ¼ inch of water in a pot and bring to a boil. Add tofu, and cover pot.
2. Reduce flame to low, and simmer 1–2 minutes. Remove tofu, drain, and place on individual serving plates.
3. Prepare a sauce by mixing ½ cup water with soy sauce and grated ginger.
4. Top each slice of boiled tofu with a teaspoon of sauce, and garnish with minced parsley.

BOILED TOFU WITH TAMARI, GINGER, AND SCALLIONS

SERVES 4–5

Water
2 1-pound cakes firm tofu, quartered
Soy sauce
Grated ginger
Sliced scallions

1. Place a small amount of cold water in a saucepan. Place on a medium-low flame, and add tofu.
2. Heat the water slowly to keep the tofu soft. If you use a high flame, the tofu will harden.
3. When tofu is warmed, place one or two pieces on each plate. Garnish each piece of tofu with a couple of drops of soy sauce, a pinch of ginger, and a few scallion slices. Serve.

GINGER-GARLIC TOFU

SERVES 4

1 pound firm tofu, cut into ½-inch cubes
½ cup water
1 tablespoon soy sauce
1 teaspoon grated ginger
2 tablespoons diced onion
2 cloves garlic, minced

1. Combine all ingredients in a 2-quart or larger saucepan. Bring to boil, lower heat, and simmer for 15–20 minutes. This allows tofu to absorb all the seasonings.
2. Add a little water if liquid mixture dries out too quickly.
3. Serve warm or cool by itself; mix with vegetables, grains, or salads; or add to sandwiches, soups, or casseroles.

SERVES 4–6   # *TOFU IN BLACK BEAN SAUCE*

3 tablespoons peanut or light sesame oil
5 cloves garlic, finely chopped
1 tablespoon ginger, finely grated
3 tablespoons Chinese black beans
3 onions, coarsely chopped
2 tablespoons soy sauce
2 tablespoons barley or rice malt, or 2 teaspoons honey
2 cups water
3 tablespoons kuzu, dissolved in ⅓ cup water
1 pound firm tofu, sliced
2 teaspoons dark sesame oil

1. In a wok, heat oil until nearly smoking.
2. Add garlic and ginger, and stir-fry rapidly over high heat for 1 minute.
3. Add black beans, and stir for 30 seconds. Add onions, and stir for 2–3 minutes.
4. Add soy sauce, sweetener, and water. Bring to a boil.
5. Add kuzu. Stir with a wooden spoon until it thickens and becomes clear and shiny.
6. Stir in tofu and dark sesame oil, and simmer 2–3 minutes. Serve on rice with blanched Chinese greens.

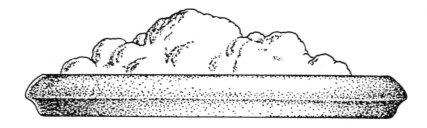

DESSERTS

FRUIT CRÊPES

SERVES 6

CRÊPES
2 cups soy milk
5 ounces silken tofu
1 teaspoon vanilla
½ teaspoon salt
2 teaspoons baking powder
1 tablespoon sweetener
2 cups pastry flour

FILLING
1 pound soft tofu
2 teaspoons lemon or orange rind, grated
2 cups strawberries, peaches, cherries, or your favorite fruit
¼ cup sweetener
⅛ teaspoon salt
¼ cup brandy or Japanese mirin (optional)

TOFU WHIPPED CRÈME
½ pound soft tofu
1 teaspoon vanilla
1 teaspoon lemon or orange rind, grated
¼ cup water plus 1 teaspoon corn oil
¼ cup sweetener
Few drops almond or anise extract

1. Mix soy milk, tofu, vanilla, salt, baking powder, and sweetener in a blender.
2. Add liquid mixture to 2 cups pastry flour. Beat only enough to combine.
3. Heat a small, lightly oiled skillet.
4. Add a small amount of batter to skillet, and spread thin by tipping pan. Cook over medium heat, turning crêpe when underside is browned.

5. To make filling, blend all filling ingredients until smooth. Set aside.
6. To make tofu whipped cream, blend all ingredients until smooth. Set aside.
7. To assemble crêpes, spread 3 tablespoons of filling on each crêpe, roll crêpe, and place on plate with seam side down. Crêpes may be served with additional fruit slices on top and/or with Tofu Whipped Crème.

SERVES 8–10

BOSTON BROWN BREAD

1 pound silken tofu
½ cup soy milk (or dairy milk)
¾ cup sweetener
1 cup cornmeal
1 cup rye flour
1 cup whole-wheat flour
1 teaspoon salt
2 teaspoons baking soda
1 cup raisins
½ cup walnuts (optional)

1. In blender, mix tofu, soy milk, and sweetener until smooth.
2. In bowl, combine cornmeal, rye flour, whole-wheat flour, salt, baking soda, and raisins. You may add walnuts at this time.
3. Add wet ingredients to dry ingredients, and mix well.
4. Pour batter into 2 oiled 1-quart pudding molds.
5. Steam 3 hours in 1 inch of water in a covered pot; or pressure cook 15 minutes without pressure, then 30 minutes at 15 pounds pressure (place about 2 cups of water on the bottom of the pressure cooker).
6. Cool before cutting (if you can wait).

APPLESAUCE CAKE

1 pound soft tofu
2 cups applesauce
½ cup vegetable oil
¼ cup sweetener
1 tablespoon lemon juice
1 tablespoon grated lemon rind
½ teaspoon cinnamon
½ teaspoon salt
2 cups whole-wheat flour
1½ teaspoons baking powder
1 cup raisins
½ cup sunflower seeds or chopped nuts

1. Blend tofu, applesauce, vegetable oil, sweetener, lemon juice, lemon rind, cinnamon, and salt until smooth.
2. In bowl, sift flour and baking powder together, then stir in liquid mixture.
3. Stir in raisins and sunflower seeds.
4. Bake in bread pan in preheated oven at 350°F for 50 minutes.

WAFFLES

½ pound soft tofu
1½ cups soy milk
2 tablespoons vegetable oil
2 teaspoons vanilla
¼ teaspoon almond extract
1 teaspoon lemon or orange rind, grated
2½ cups wheat flour
½ teaspoon salt
½ teaspoon cinnamon
½ teaspoon nutmeg
4 teaspoons baking powder
2 egg whites, whipped (optional)

1. Blend tofu, soy milk, vegetable oil, vanilla, almond extract, and lemon or orange rind until smooth. Set aside.

2. In bowl, mix flour, salt, cinnamon, nutmeg, and baking powder.
3. Mix wet ingredients with dry ingredients, fold in egg whites if desired, and cook in a well-oiled waffle iron.

SERVES 4

APRICOT ALMOND PIE

ALMOND CRUST
1 cup ground almonds
1 cup pastry flour
⅛ cup vegetable oil
⅛ cup sweetener
2 ounces silken tofu

FILLING
1½ pounds soft tofu
½ cup soy milk
½ cup sweetener
1 teaspoon vanilla
¼ teaspoon almond extract

APRICOT TOPPING
1 cup dried apricots
2 cups apple cider
¼ teaspoon cinnamon
¼ cup flaked coconut
¼ cup sweetener
⅛ cup brandy or amaretto (optional)

1. For crust, mix all crust ingredients. Press into pie plate, and bake in preheated oven at 400°F for 10 minutes.
2. For filling, blend all filling ingredients until smooth. Pour mixture into baked pie shell, and bake in preheated oven at 325°F for 1 hour, or until firm.
3. For topping, blend first four topping ingredients, and simmer in pot for 30 minutes.
4. Blend cooked filling with sweetener and, if you wish, with brandy or amaretto.
5. Pour topping over pie. Chill, and serve.

PINEAPPLE PIE

SERVES 4

1½ pounds silken tofu
½ cup sweetener
2 tablespoons vegetable oil
1 teaspoon vanilla
2 teaspoons lemon or orange rind, grated
16-ounce can unsweetened crushed pineapple (reserve juice)
¼ cup shredded or flaked coconut
9-inch prebaked pie shell

1. Blend tofu, sweetener, oil, vanilla, lemon rind, pineapple, and enough of the pineapple juice to facilitate blending until smooth. (Mixing half at a time will make blending easier.)
2. Fold in coconut, pour into pie shell, and chill for 2 hours before serving.

EGGLESS LEMON PIE

SERVES 4

2 cups water
⅔ cup sweetener
⅓ cup cornstarch or arrowroot
¾ pound silken tofu
½ cup lemon juice
2 teaspoons grated lemon rind
¼ teaspoon nutmeg
9-inch baked pie shell

1. Mix together water, sweetener, and cornstarch or arrowroot.
2. Cook until thick and smooth, stirring constantly.
3. Add tofu, lemon juice, lemon rind, and nutmeg.
4. Cook until very hot, but not boiling.
5. Pour into baked pie shell. Chill. Serve topped with whipped cream or Tofu Whipped Crème. (See recipe on page 147.)

SERVES 4

PUMPKIN PIE

3 cups pumpkin (or hubbard squash), cooked
1 pound soft tofu
¾ teaspoon sweetener
1 teaspoon salt
1 teaspoon cinnamon
½ teaspoon ginger
½ teaspoon powdered cloves
2 eggs (optional)
2 teaspoons orange rind, grated (optional)
1 tablespoon vanilla
Prebaked 9-inch pie shell

1. Using an electric mixer or food processor, combine all filling ingredients.
2. Pour mixture into pie shell, and bake for 1 hour at 350°F in preheated oven.

SERVES 8

ORANGE CHIFFON PIE

CRUST
½ cup rolled oats
1 cup wheat flour
¼ cup vegetable oil
2 ounces soft tofu
¼ cup coconut
½ teaspoon salt
2 tablespoons water

FILLING
1 pound soft tofu
½ cup sweetener
¼ cup orange juice concentrate
2 teaspoons grated orange rind
¼ teaspoon salt
2 egg whites
1 orange, cut into sections, or ½ cup mandarin oranges
Orange sections (for decoration)

1. To make crust, combine all ingredients in large bowl and mix. Press into oiled 9-inch pie plate. Bake 10 minutes at 400°F in preheated oven.
2. Blend tofu, sweetener, concentrate, rind, and salt until smooth.
3. Place in bowl and fold in egg whites.
4. Carefully fold in orange sections.
5. Pour into baked pie shell, and bake for 1 hour at 325°F.
6. Chill. Serve with additional orange sections on top.

CHESTNUT CRÈME PIE

SERVES 4

9-inch pie shell

FILLING
1 pound chestnut meats
1 pound soft tofu
½ cup sweetener
2 tablespoons vegetable oil
1 teaspoon vanilla
⅛ cup brandy (optional)
Pinch salt
½ cup soy milk
Few drops anise extract (optional)

TOPPING
½ pound soft tofu
1 teaspoon vanilla
¼ cup sweetener
¼ cup soy milk
Anise extract (optional)

1. To make filling, cover chestnut meats with water and simmer for 45 minutes; drain.
2. In blender or food processor, blend chestnuts and other filling ingredients until smooth.
3. Pour mixture into pie shell, and bake for 1 hour in 325°F preheated oven.
4. Blend topping ingredients until smooth, pour over pie, chill, and serve.

TOFU CHEESECAKE

SERVES 4

CRUST
¼ cup vegetable oil
4 tablespoons sweetener
¼ teaspoon salt
1½ cups wheat flour

CHEESECAKE FILLING
1½–2 pounds soft tofu
4 tablespoons tahini
1 tablespoon lemon juice
3 tablespoons cornstarch or arrowroot
½ cup sweetener
2 teaspoons vanilla
1 teaspoon salt
Grated rind of 1 lemon
Fruit for topping (optional)

1. To make crust, beat vegetable oil, sweetener, and salt in a bowl until well blended.
2. Add flour, and mix well with a fork.
3. Turn into the center of an oiled 9-inch pie plate. Press crust into pie plate and bake in preheated oven at 375°F for 8 minutes.
4. To make filling, crumble tofu into blender. Add all remaining ingredients, and blend well.
5. Pour tofu mixture into crust, and bake in preheated oven at 350°F for 35 to 40 minutes.
6. Cool first, then add your favorite fruit topping if desired.

STRAWBERRY KIWI CHEESECAKE SERVES 8

NUT CRUST
½ cup almonds or almond meal
1½ cups rolled oats
½ cup whole-wheat flour
½ teaspoon sea salt
¼ cup safflower oil
Few tablespoons apple juice to bind

FILLING
3 eggs
½–¾ cup maple syrup
2 pounds soft tofu
2 tablespoons lemon rind
Juice of 1 lemon
½ teaspoon sea salt
2 teaspoons vanilla
2 tablespoons arrowroot flour
¼ cup carob or cocoa powder

TOPPING
1–2 kiwi fruits, peeled and sliced
½ pound fresh strawberries, hulled and sliced
1 cup roasted walnuts, crushed

1. To make crust, roast almonds until lightly browned, then grind until very fine.
2. Add rolled oats, and blend together until oats are mealy.
3. Add flour, salt, and oil, and blend quickly.
4. Slowly drip in apple juice until mixture begins to bind together.
5. Oil an 8-inch spring form pan, and press or roll crust on bottom only.
6. Bake in a preheated oven at 375°F for 20 minutes, or until firm.
7. Meanwhile, separate eggs. Put yolks and syrup in blender, and whip until creamy.
8. Add tofu to egg mixture, beating well.
9. Then, add rest of ingredients except arrowroot and carob powder.

10. Divide the mixture in half.
11. Stir the carob powder into one half.
12. Then, stir the arrowroot into each half and set aside.
13. Beat egg whites until peaked, and divide between the two mixtures. Fold into each half gently. Spoon the plain mixture into the pie shell, alternating with the carob-flavored one.
14. Bake 30–40 minutes, or until cake is almost firm to the touch.
15. Turn oven off, but leave cake in oven to cool with oven door slightly ajar.
16. Remove collar of pan, and press crushed nuts around the sides.
17. Arrange kiwi slices in center of cake around fresh strawberry slices. If any strawberries are left over, position them around edge of cake. Serve quickly to preserve the look of the fresh fruit.

SERVES 4

TROPICAL CHEESECAKE

Graham cracker or pastry pie crust

FILLING
1 pound soft tofu
2 ripe bananas
2 eggs (optional)
1 teaspoon vanilla
⅓ cup sweetener
1 cup crushed pineapple, drained

TOPPING
1 cup orange juice
½ cup pineapple juice
¼ cup soft tofu
2 tablespoons sweetener
4 teaspoons cornstarch or arrowroot

1. To make filling, blend tofu, bananas, eggs, vanilla, and sweetener until smooth.

2. Pour mixture into a bowl, and stir in pineapple.
3. Turn mixture into pie or graham cracker crust, and bake in preheated oven at 350°F for 35–45 minutes.
4. For topping, blend all ingredients until smooth.
5. In a saucepan, cook mixture over low heat, stirring constantly, until thick.
6. Spread topping over the baked Tropical Cheesecake, and allow to cool before serving.

RICE PUDDING

SERVES 4

1 pound silken tofu
2 eggs (optional)
½ cup sweetener
2 tablespoons lemon juice
½ cup soy milk
4 teaspoons vegetable oil
½ teaspoon salt
¼ teaspoon cinnamon
½ teaspoon nutmeg
2 teaspoons vanilla
1 teaspoon grated lemon rind
2 cups cooked rice
½ cup shredded coconut (optional)
½ cup raisins or chopped dates

1. In blender, mix tofu, eggs, sweetener, lemon juice, soy milk, vegetable oil, salt, cinnamon, nutmeg, vanilla, and lemon rind until smooth.
2. Pour mixture into bowl. Add rice, coconut, and raisins or dates, and mix well.
3. Bake in an oiled dish at 350°F for about 50 minutes. Serve hot or cold.

SERVES 4

CHOCOLATE PUDDING

1 pound silken tofu
3 tablespoons unsweetened chocolate, melted
Grated rind from ¼ lemon or ½ orange
Juice from ½ lemon or orange
2 tablespoons honey
½ teaspoon vanilla extract

1. Blend all ingredients, and pour into individual serving dishes.
2. Refrigerate before serving.

SERVES 4

INDIAN PUDDING

2 cups water
1 cup cornmeal
¾ cup sweetener
¼ cup vegetable oil
1 teaspoon salt
1 pound silken tofu
1 teaspoon ginger
1½ teaspoons vanilla
½ teaspoon cinnamon (optional)

1. Cook water and cornmeal in pot for 20–25 minutes, stirring occasionally.
2. Add remaining ingredients and mix in blender until smooth.
3. Bake in an oiled dish for 1 hour at 350°F in preheated oven. Serve hot.

TOFU CHOCOLATE CHIP COOKIES

MAKES ABOUT
16 COOKIES

1½ cups pastry flour
¾ teaspoon baking powder
½ teaspoon salt
6 ounces chocolate or carob chips
½ cup chopped nuts
¾ cup sweetener
½ cup vegetable oil
½ pound soft tofu
1 egg (optional)
1 teaspoon vanilla

1. In bowl, mix flour, baking powder, salt, chocolate, and nuts. Set aside.
2. In blender, purée remaining ingredients.
3. Mix the liquid into the dry ingredients.
4. Drop mixture by spoonfuls onto oiled cookie sheets.
5. Preheat oven to 400°F. Bake 10 minutes, or until golden brown.

TOFU COCONUT COOKIES

MAKES ABOUT
16 COOKIES

1½ cups pastry flour
¾ teaspoon baking powder
½ teaspoon salt
1 cup shredded coconut
½ cup chopped nuts or sunflower seeds
¾ cup sweetener
½ cup vegetable oil
½ pound soft tofu
1 egg (optional)
1 teaspoon vanilla

1. In large bowl, mix flour, baking powder, salt, coconut, and nuts.

2.   In blender, purée remaining ingredients.
3.   Mix the liquid into the dry ingredients.
4.   Drop mixture by spoonfuls onto oiled cookie sheets.
5.   Preheat oven to 400°F. Bake 10 minutes, or until golden brown.

MAKES ONE
QUART

TOFU ICE CREAM

2 tablespoons raw sugar
⅛ cup silken tofu
2 teaspoons lemon or orange rind
½ cup soy milk
1 pound strawberries or any other favorite fruit or flavoring

1.   Place all ingredients in blender; blend until smooth.
2.   If you have an ice cream machine, pour liquid in; it will take about 30 minutes to freeze.
3.   If you don't have an ice cream machine, place mixture on a flat tray in the freezer. When partially frozen, take mixture out and beat until ice crystals break up. Return to freezer, beat once more, and then leave it to set. Serve.

Conclusion

I n *Holidays à la Heart*, the sixth edition of a yearly publication put out by the American Heart Association (AHA), there are recipes for some mouth-watering traditional seasonal favorites, like Holiday Turkey Breast, Sweet Potato Cups, Peach Cake, and Hot Spicy Cider.

Tofu proved to be an important guest at the AHA's holiday party. Hot Raisin Spice Pudding and Holiday Deviled Un-Eggs—each using tofu as a main ingredient—were selected by the AHA as two of only twelve holiday recipes presented in its seasonal pamphlet of heart-healthy meals.

This highlights just how popular tofu has become, and how by doing so it has fulfilled many people's expectations. In the late 1970s, futurists said that tofu would prove to be the "yogurt of the 1980s" by changing from an obscure, foreign food into a multimillion-dollar health food phenomenon. They also said that before tofu could prosper, the public would have to view it as an Americanized product. Well, tofu probably couldn't get much more Americanized than it already has. It has taken the form of everything from the all-American hot dog to goodies like gourmet chocolates, mints, and ice cream-type products, as well as being an ingredient in down-home comfort foods like hearty pot pies.

Because of all these new products and the subsequent increased public awareness of tofu, sales in the early 1990s are expected to hit $500 million, according to *Health Foods Business Magazine*. This isn't surprising, since tofu sales tripled between 1978 and 1988. Currently, approximately 65 million pounds of tofu are produced and consumed yearly in the United States.

Obviously, things have changed quite a bit since Sing Hau Lee opened one of the United States' first tofu shops around the turn of the century. In the last eleven years alone, John and his brother-in-law have found a wide-open market for their tofu innovations from Nasoya. Now, there are almost two hundred tofu manufacturers in the country.

Why are these tofu manufacturers so busy? Because tofu has become an irreplaceable staple in many families' diets.

Cancer. Heart disease. We've seen these—our country's biggest killers—linked irrefutably to what we eat. We have been warned of these correlations for quite some time, but studies show that the information gathered is now being taken to heart.

For example, according to studies reported by the California Dietetic Association, nine out of ten women born between 1946 and 1964 have changed their habits of buying food because of their concern over nutrition and diet-related diseases. Since many of these consumers are shopping not only for themselves but for their growing children as well, it seems hopeful that a whole generation may be growing up on healthful, cholesterol-fighting foods like tofu.

And it isn't just those concerned with personal health who embrace tofu and soy foods. It's also those concerned—as so many of us are—with the health of the world's population and the planet itself. When we hear about tens of thousands of people—many of them children—starving to death each year all over the world, many of us know that one of the main hopes for the future is the soybean and foods made from it.

The California Vegetarian Association (CVA) has stated that it doesn't believe that the current world population can maintain itself on a meat-based diet indefinitely. Like many environmentally concerned activists, this group feels that the waste and inefficiency involved in meat production will not sustain the planet into the twenty-first century.

Vegetable protein, for example, requires just one-tenth of the land that animal protein does. In addition, the CVA points out that a vegetarian diet requires one-thirteenth the amount of water needed to produce animal protein. The CVA also states that 90 percent of the country's grain goes to feed livestock. Interestingly, decreasing meat production by just 10 percent would make enough grain available to feed 60 million people. It's wonderful to know that we can cut our cholesterol and calories with tofu lasagna, pizza, meatballs, or cheesecake, all the while enjoying a food that is playing an increasingly important role in world health.

Famed *New York Times* nutrition writer Jane Brody has pointed out that although soy food sales are skyrocketing, the food still has much potential. "The soybean may be the single most important food produced in the world today. It is certainly the most versatile," she has written. "But its potential as a nourishing and delicious food far exceeds its current role."

Most of the soybeans grown in the United States—the world leader in soybean production—are exported or fed to livestock. Soybeans, however, are the main source of protein in much of Asia. Because of their importance, soybeans have been called the "cow of China."

It's clear, though, that the West is in a soy—and especially a tofu—revolution. The 1990s will clearly be the decade during which tofu becomes an accepted, mainstream Western food.

After trying our nutrition-packed recipes for chili, guacamole, tofu parmigiana, cheesecake, strawberry mousse, and pineapple pie, you may find that tofu has become one of the most popular and requested guests in your pantry.

Mail-Order Natural Foods

The following companies are only some of the many sources of natural foods that can be obtained through the mail. Write or call them directly for catalogs or further information.

American Spoon Foods
411 E. Lake Street
Petoskey, MI 49770

(616) 347-9030

Diamond K Enterprises
RR1, Box 30
St. Charles, MN 55972

(507) 932-4308

Frontier Cooperative Herbs
P.O. Box 299
Norway, IA 52318

(319) 227-7991

Garden Spot Distributors
Route 1, Box 729A
New Holland, PA 17557

(717) 354-4936

Jaffe Bros.
P.O. Box 636
Valley Center, CA 92082

(619) 749-1133

Kushi Foundation
P.O. Box 1100
Brookline Village, MA 02147

(617) 738-0045

Living Farms
Box 50
Tracy, MN 56175

(800) 533-5320

Mountain Ark Trading Co.
120 S. East Street
Fayetteville, AR 72701

(800) 643-8909

Neshaminy Valley Natural
Foods
421 Pike Road
Huntingdon Valley, PA 19006

(215) 364-8440

Smile Herb Shop
4908 Berwyn Road
College Park, MD 20740

(301) 474-4288

Timber Crest Farms
4791 Dry Creek Road
Healdsburg, CA 95448

(707) 433-8351

Walnut Acres
Penn's Creek, PA 17862

(717) 837-0601

Bibliography

American Institute of Health and Nutrition. *Journey for Health*. Lakeland, FL: Foster and McNeil, Inc., 1985.

Anderson, Juel. *Juel Anderson's Tofu Kitchen*. New York: Bantam Books, 1982.

Brody, Jane. *Jane Brody's Good Food Book*. New York: W. W. Norton and Company, 1985.

Downes, John. *Soy Source*. Dorset, England: Prism Press, 1987.

Editors of *East West Journal*. *Shopper's Guide to Natural Foods*. Garden City Park, NY: Avery Publishing Group, 1987.

Hagler, Louise. *Tofu Quick and Easy*. Summertown, TN: The Book Publishing Company, 1986.

Heidenry, Carolyn. *Making the Transition to a Macrobiotic Diet*. Garden City Park, NY: Avery Publishing Group, 1984.

Lambert, Junko. *The Tofu Cookbook*. San Francisco: Chronicle Books, 1983.

Leviton, Richard. *Tofu, Tempeh, Miso and Other Soyfoods: The "Food of the Future."* New Canaan, CT: Keats Publishing, Inc., 1982.

Mitchell, Paulette. *The New American Vegetarian Menu Cookbook*. Emmaus, PA: Rodale Press, 1984.

Paino, John. *Nasoya Tofu Cookbook*. Leominster, MA: Okara Press, 1987.

Shurtleff, William and Akiko Aoyagi. *The Book of Kudzu*. Garden City Park, NY: Avery Publishing Group, 1985.

Shurtleff, William and Akiko Aoyagi. *The Book of Tofu*. Berkeley, CA: Ten Speed Press, 1975.

Shurtleff, William and Akiko Aoyagi. *History of Tofu*. Lafayette, CA: Soyfoods Center, 1983.

Weber, Marcea. *Naturally Sweet Desserts*. Garden City Park, NY: Avery Publishing Group, 1990.

Index